The Arab Nation

Samir Amin

OTHER BOOKS BY SAMIR AMIN (in English)

Accumulation on a World Scale: a Critique of the Theory
of Underdevelopment, (Monthly Review, 1974)
Maghreb in the Modern World, (Penguin, 1971)
Modern Migrations in Western Africa, (O.U.P., 1974)
Neo-colonialism in West Africa, (Penguin, 1974)
Unequal Development: Social Formations at the Periphery
of the Capitalist System, (Monthly Review, 1976)

The Arab Nation

Samir Amin

Translated by Michael Pallis

Zed Press Ltd., 57 Caledonian Road, London N1 9DN.

The Arab Nation was first published in English by Zed Press,
57 Caledonian Road, London N1 9DN in June 1978.

Copyright © Les Editions de Minuit 1976
Translation Copyright © Zed Press 1978

ISBN: Hb 0 905762 22 3
      Pb 0 905762 23 1

Printed by Billing & Sons Ltd., London
Typeset by Lyn Caldwell
Designed by An Dekker

CONTENTS

FOREWORD

There are six main theses in this book which clash with opinions current among Arab Marxists.

The first of these theses suggests that the pre-colonial Arab world was not feudal, that it constituted a constellation of social formations articulated around a tributary mode of production. The latter was relatively prosperous in Egypt and relatively poor elsewhere — with a few exceptions such as Iraq from the 8th to the 10th century — due to the weak development of the agricultural forces of production in this predominantly arid and semi-arid area. This thesis is completed by another which asserts that during the great periods of Arab civilization a predominant role was played by trade relations, both external (long distance trade) and internal (grafted on to the former).

The second thesis relates to the theory of the nation. We maintain that Arab unity was the historical product of the mercantile integration of the Arab world, as carried out by a class of merchant-warriors. It was only with the decline of trade relations that national disintegration set in, a disintegration which was accentuated by integration of the Arab world into the imperialist system. At the same time imperialist domination transposed the Arab feeling of unity on to another level. This feeling is now mainly one of struggle against a common enemy. Naturally, none of the dominant Arab classes of the imperialist era (the comprador and latifundist bourgeoisies, and then the state bourgeoisie), are capable of bringing this Arab unity to its fruition.

The third thesis touches on imperialism and its class alliance in the Arab world. We suggest that, at first, imperialism allies itself with classes, engendered by its own development, which benefit from the integration of their country into the world system. These classes are the comprador bourgeoisie and the big landowners; furthermore the latter should not really be described as feudal; we shall refer to them as a latifundist bourgeoisie, to underline the transformation imposed on them by the dominant capitalism. During the first period of the alliance, the national bourgeoisie is more a potentiality than a present reality. Later, however, the bourgeoisie forces imperialism to accept the new modalities of the international division of labour, which enables this bourgeoisie to develop and to become the main ally of imperialism. Agrarian reforms engender a new class, somewhat similar to the kulaks, which turns into the rural branch of this new international class alliance. The main form taken by the bourgeoisie during this second stage is a statist one. There can then be no question of its leading the way along a 'non-capitalist' road: the bourgeoisie has already become the strategic ally of imperialism.

The fourth thesis concerns the petty bourgeoisie. The proletariat and the poorer peasantry having given over the leadership of the anti-imperialist struggle to the petty bourgeoisie — which then opposes the first generation collaborationist bourgeoisie — there are no obstacles to the development of a new form of exploitation, dependent state capitalism. Far from committing suicide as a class, the petty bourgeoisie engenders a state bourgeoisie each time it assumes the leadership of the anti-imperialist movement.

The fifth thesis bears on the role of the USSR and the Soviet-Arab Alliance. We maintain that the failure of the communist organisations, allied to the poor peasantry, is the direct outcome of the fact that these organisations toe the Moscow line based on support for state bourgeoisies. These errors expose the predominantly petty bourgeois character of Arab communism. In fact this opportunist line is linked to the aims of the Soviet Union, aims which are those of a new class society and a new super power. The distortion of Marxism which this strategy involves ruins any chances for an effective revolutionary strategy. Whatever arguments there may be for an alliance with the Soviet Union, in order to face up to the main enemy, in this case Western and especially American imperialism, a lucid analysis of the new situation brought about by the internal evolution of the USSR is the preliminary condition of any correct action.

The sixth thesis deals with Arab unity. This unity, which is above all that of the people (proletariat, poorer peasantry, uncorrupted strata of the petty bourgeoisie and intellectuals) against imperialism, must first be a recognition of diversity.

We have not been willing to sacrifice the assertion of essential strategic points of view to the demands of tactical considerations (existing political alliances in this or that concrete situation). On the other hand, we must ask the reader not to lose sight of the thrust of our criticisms by isolating this or that statement from the global context and perspective.

For it is strategic errors which explain the failure, so far, of revolution in the Arab world: failure in Egypt where all the objective conditions for revolution have existed for over a century, in a country which is in so many ways so similar to China and Vietnam; failure in Palestine, hot spot of the anti-imperialist struggle for thirty years.

Naturally, the raising of these questions implies the need for deep theoretical revisions, touching on the Marxist conception itself. Since the present book deals specifically with the Arab world, we refer the reader to the general works in which these basic theoretical issues are developed. These works are primarily *Unequal Development* and *L'imperialisme et le developpement inegal*[1] in which the reader will find: 1) the theory of the tributary mode of production and that of long distance trade; 2) the theory of the nation; 3) the theory of imperialism, of its stages and of the class alliances which characterise it; 4) the theory of the formation of a world system; 5) the theory of unequal exchange and asymmetric development under the imperialist system; 6) the theory of the subordination of agriculture to capitalism, and the theory of the transformations in the nature of peasant modes of production and in the patterns of land ownership which are linked to it; 7) the theory of the present crisis of imperialism; 8) the critique of the economicist reduction of Marxism and the analysis of the economicist distortions of Soviet Marxism — notably its mechanistic vision of the relationship between the forces of production and the relations of production, its reduction of socialism to a capitalism without capitalists, its strategy for the transition period, its vision of the problem of technology and of models of consumption adopted from the bourgeoisie, etc.; 9) the theory of the Soviet mode of production.

We also recommend to the reader *L'Egypte masserienne* and *La lutte de classes en Egypte*, which we have drawn on for our critiques of the 19th century Nahda nationalist movement in Egypt, of the nationalist party, of the Wafd and of Nasserism. We have also drawn on *The Maghreb in the Modern World* for the analysis of the North African liberation movements.[2]

Finally we assume that the reader has a rough idea of Arab history and has followed some of the latest developments.

1

THE HISTORICAL FOUNDATIONS OF ARAB NATIONALISM

PROLOGUE

Arab public opinion is extremely sensitive to everything which goes on in Palestine. What could be more natural? From the Atlantic shores of Morocco to the Persian Gulf, from the Mediterranean to the centre of the Sahara and to the upper Nile, a hundred million people speak the same language, listen to the same radio programmes, read the same books and see the same films. They have all been oppressed by the same European imperialism during the contemporary period. Nevertheless, when one asks one of them: 'What is your nationality?' not one will spontaneously answer 'Arab'; the reply will be 'Moroccan', 'Egyptian', 'Yemenite', etc. Do these hundred million people form one nation, the Arab nation, as the contemporary ideologues of Arab nationalism assert — even granted that this nation is still in the course of formation? Or do they make up fifteen different, albeit related, nations, as orthodox communism has long claimed? Is the attachment to Palestine only a sentimental one, or is it based on a consciousness of political solidarity against imperialism and Israel? The question of the nation in the Arab world is not a question of dogma — be it Marxist or bourgeois; nor is it an unimportant issue which only serves to mask the fundamental problems of liberation from imperialist exploitation. For the framework in which the class struggle unfolds is a national framework and the oppression suffered by the people of the area is not just economic but also national.

We have grown used to confusing the existence of nations with one of its expressions, the one which results from the history of Europe, where relatively homogeneous, administratively and politically centralised nation states progressively constituted themselves and were economically united by the development of capitalism. When these nations were constituting themselves, the bourgeoisie played the decisive role: that of a unifying ruling class producing a dominant ideology. The definition given by Stalin of the five conditions for nationhood sum up this historical experience.

When one goes beyond the European field one notices the inadequacy of the concepts on which the Stalinist theory of the nation was based. The theory assumes that the nation is a social phenomenon produced by capitalism, or rather by indigenous capitalism, since it is indigenous capitalism which founds the nation.

According to these assumptions, nations would only exist at the centre of the world capitalist system, in the areas where the bourgeois revolution has established the national power of the local bourgeoisie. Elsewhere nations would not actually exist, at least not in a finished form. What then are we to say of the social realities of the pre-capitalist world, where an old statist tradition blends into a cultural and linguistic reality? Thousand year old Egypt has always been united on the level of language, of culture and — except during some brief periods of decadence — on the level of political power as well. Whilst it is not a bourgeois nation, it is certainly something more than an incongruous and unorganised conglomerate of peoples. Furthermore, even those regions which were not organised into unified and centralised states, and which were not united culturally and linguistically, have increasingly become so following upon their integration into the international capitalist system as colonies or as dominated semi-dependent countries. Even if this unification has not been the work of a national bourgeoisie it is nonetheless an important social fact. What does this point of view tell us about the structure and definition of the Arab world? The Arab world stretches over several thousand miles within that semi-arid area, the midriff of the Old World, which reaches from the Atlantic to tropical Asia. It occupies a specific part of the area, isolated from Europe by the Mediterranean, from Black Africa by the Sahara, from the Turkish and Persian worlds by the mountains of the Taurus, of Kurdistan and of Western Iran. This Arab world is not exactly congruent with the Muslim World. The latter occupies almost all of the semi-arid area shared by four peoples (the Arabs, the Turks, the Persians and the Indo-Afghani's), overspills a little into tropical Asia (Bengal, Indonesia) and, more recently, into certain areas of Black Africa (West and East Africa). Nor can the Arab world be reduced to some or other ethno-racial phenomenon, for Arabisation has mixed together many peoples with different origins and different racial components. It was a relatively centralised political entity only during a very brief period of its history: two centuries. And even then, at the time of the Ommayids and the first Abbassids, from 750 to 950, linguistic unification was far less advanced than it is today. After 950 the Arab world exploded into relatively stable regional political entities which were only to be reunited, and superficially at that, under Ottoman rule.

Is the Arab world then only a grouping of peoples speaking closely related languages? Were this so, the Arabic spoken languages would surely have evolved towards a growing differentiation, just as from a common Latin core the romance languages have evolved to become today's French, Spanish and Italian. But the evolutionary trend of the Arab languages is headed in precisely the opposite direction: the literary language is tending to become the spoken language of the whole of the Arab world.

It is in this complex and evolving national framework that the class struggle and anti-imperialist liberation struggle unfolds. It is in this framework that we must re-situate the Palestinian question.

THE VARIOUS AREAS OF THE PRE-COLONIAL ARAB WORLD

The pre-colonial social formations of the Arab world were far from sharing the same structure. The image of a rural and feudal Arab world is as widespread, among both foreigners and Arab Marxists, as it is unscientific. In fact the Arab world cannot be assimilated to Mediaeval Europe. Furthermore, it has always been possible to differentiate it into three zones, distinguished by social structure or by political and economic organisation. First, there is the Arab East (in Arabic, Al Mashreq) which includes Arabia, Syria (that is to say today's states of Syria, Lebanon, Jordan and Israel) and Iraq. Secondly, there are the countries of the Nile, Egypt and the Sudan. Finally, there is the Arab West (Al Maghreb) which stretches from Libya to the Atlantic and includes today's Libya, Tunisia, Algeria, Morocco and Mauritania. Of all these only Egypt, in the middle of the Arab world, has always been a peasant civilisation. Elsewhere rural life was precarious, the techniques of agricultural production were underdeveloped, the productivity of agricultural work was low, the standard of living of the rural world was close to the subsistence level and, therefore, the forms of social organisation of this world were necessarily marked by a primitive collectivism. There was certainly no basis here for the appropriation of the sort of surplus which allows for a brilliant civilisation. Nonetheless — and this paradox is the source of a great many misunderstandings about the Arab world — the Mashreq, and to some extent the Maghreb, developed rich and specifically urban civilisations. The central question, here as always, is: where did the surplus on which these civilisations were built come from?

To understand the Arab world, one must see it in its own context, as a stop-over area, as a turntable between the main areas of civilisation of the Old World. This semi-arid zone separates three areas whose civilisations were essentially agrarian: Europe, Black Africa, Tropical Asia. The Arab zone fulfilled commercial functions, bringing together agrarian worlds which otherwise had little contact with one another. The social formations on which the flowering of its civilisations was based were essentially trading formations. By this we mean that the crucial surplus which was the lifeblood of its great cities at their height did not come mainly from the exploitation of its rural world. On the contrary, this surplus came from the profits of its long distance trade, profits guaranteed by the Arab world's monopoly of its function of intermediary. In the last analysis this income came from the surplus appropriated from the peasantries of other countries by the ruling classes of those countries. In turn Arab commercial prosperity affected Arab agricultural development, and enabled it to progress significantly, at least in certain areas and at certain times.

This model of a trading formation was characteristic of the Mashreq until the end of the 1914-1918 War, when the integration of this area of the Arab world into the imperialist sector caused major changes in the Iraqi class structure, and minor ones in Syria and Palestine.

This is an important point to remember when we come to analyse the behaviour of the bourgeoisie of this Arab East vis-a-vis French, English, and then American imperialism, and its attitude to the Palestinian problem. In the Maghreb the type of formation we have been describing was characteristic of the area until colonisation by the French. But the latter, both older and deeper than the colonisation which was imposed on the Mashreq, brought crucial changes to the modern Maghreb. Between the two areas, Egypt continued to be the exception, a tributary peasant formation integrated into the world capitalist system.

The Mashreq

Islam was born in Arabia, in the middle of the desert, among a nomadic population organised as a function of the trade between the Roman Empire and Persia on the one hand; Southern Arabia, Ethiopia and Persia on the other. It was the profits from this trade which made the urban merchant republics of the Hajaz possible. The domination of the towns over micro-areas of rural oases was far from being the main asset of the merchant ruling classes. As for the nomads' pastoral subsistence economy, it was carried on alongside the activity of the merchants, and was for the latter a source of men and beasts, but never the subject of direct surplus appropriation. The desert civilisation therefore presupposed that of the Roman East and of the tropical countries, between which it acted as a bridge. If at any stage the surplus which fed the long distance trade came, for one reason or another, to be reduced, or when the trade routes changed, the desert died. Historically this often happened, and each time the men of the desert attempted to survive by becoming conquerors, as Maxime Rodinson has shown in his analysis of the historical conditions in the 8th century.[1] It is from these origins that the marked mechant character of Islamic ideology comes from. The first region of the civilised world conquered by the Arabs was the 'fertile crescent', the countries of Syria and Iraq on the northern border of the Arabian desert. The Arabs were reasonably at home there, for the societies of the ancient East had been, like theirs, tributary merchant societies. True, there were still peasants in this semi-arid zone, despite its name, whilst to the south there were practically none. The peasants were mountain people, clinging to the slopes of Lebanon, of the Alids, of the Taurus and of Kurdistan, and dependent on a level of rainfall barely sufficient for their miserable subsistence. These rural areas were obviously far too poor to supply the surplus necessary to a brilliant civilisation. They were still primitive, organised in village communities, relatively isolated and furthermore fiercely attached to their independence. Civilisation had emerged only on the fringes of the region, in two exceptional areas: Mesopotamia and the Mediterranean seafront. Mesopotamia was the birthplace of the first real rural civilisation, thanks to the natural conditions provided by the Tigris and the Euphrates. This civilisation, similar to the Egyptian one, was based on a surplus appropriated by the cities at the expense of the countryside. Like all agricultural civilisations established on the edges of the desert, it lived under constant threat of a barbarian attack, a threat which became a reality during the Turco-Mongol invasions of the 10th and 11th centuries. Not until the 19th century did civilisation rise again in the area, and then only under the shadow of the Pax Britannica.

To the West, by the sea, the city-states of Phoenicia and Tyre drew their resources from long distance trade, both by sea and by caravan. The Arabs coming out of the desert eventually shifted the commercial civilisation of Medina northwards, making Damascus the new Ommayid capital. Having thus regained control of the trade routes, they were again able to profit from the flow of trade and thus revive their civilisation.

The Arab invasion reached out eastwards beyond the Semite and Byzantine fertile crescent, to integrate Sassanid Persia into the new Muslim state. This expansion was quite significant for the still emerging Arab world. The Abbasid Caliphate based its model of organisation on that of the Sassanid state, for instance.

For several centuries, the first and the greatest era, the frontiers of the Arab world were vague and difficult to distinguish from those of Islam. Arabisation went hand in hand with Islamisation, as the modern Persian language testifies. The urban world of Iran was strongly Arabised. The first of the new generations of philosophers and scientists born east of the Zagros, expressed themselves in Arabic and greatly influenced the formation of the new culture. The peasants, however, were not drawn into this movement. After the Turco-Mongol invasions and the decadence or outright destruction of the towns, the Iranian renaissance began to bring out the non-Arab character of the countries east of the Zagros. Not until then did the frontiers of the Arab world clearly distinguish it from the Iranian world.

The Turco-Mongol invasions did not modify these frontiers. Turkish penetration of the area was slow, and the Turks were already Islamised by the time they reached it. In the Arab lands they were satisfied to dominate the state and settled only in Anatolia, that is to say in territories which they themselves had conquered for Islam. The Mongol invasions passed over like a destructive hurricane. As for the Ottoman state it first took over from the Seljouks in Anatolia and then subordinated the whole of the Arab world, except Morocco and Southern Arabia.

The unity of the fertile crescent was not to be broken until the end of the First World War. It was a unity in diversity, but this diversity was never really cultural or ethnic. The nature of an area of this sort — the essence of which was its commercial function, the bringing together of areas around it — was to play a dialectically unifying-dislocating role. Unifying because it caused men to move around endlessly, customs and religions to spread, and a travellers' *lingua franca* to develop. Dislocatory because founded on the rivalry of merchant cities. Under these conditions, the imposition or the absence of a single formal political authority had little importance. When such a political power was strong it imposed limits on the competition of the merchant cities and often ensured the predominance of the capital. Such was the essential character of the Ommayid state, based in Damascus, then of the Abbasid state, centred on Baghdad. To ensure its power, the state relied on a mercenary army recruited amongst the neighbouring nomads. As for the peasants, they sought to keep to the isolation of their mountains, and it was only in the suburban areas that they fell into semi-servile dependence on urban or absentee landlords (merchants, courtiers, etc.). The only exception was Lower Iraq, organised into merchant-owned slave plantations on the Roman model. For twelve centuries the fertile crescent was thus united and divided; from 700 to 1900, periods of high civilisation were followed by periods of decadence, at the whim of the commercial networks linking Western and Byzantine Europe with the Indian and Chinese East.

The nuances which must be pointed out do not contradict our theses, they complement them. We are well aware that Iraq was, for several centuries, a rich agricultural area. The same is true, on a smaller scale, for Western Syria. We realize that the income which this fact afforded to the ruling classes and the state was significant. It is nonetheless the case that this development of irrigated agriculture was grafted onto an already constituted state, a state born in Medina, moved to Damascus and finally established in Baghdad. The development of agriculture was in this case more the outcome of the stability and prosperity of the Caliphate than its cause. The state retained many traces of its merchant origins, particularly at the ideological level. Thus this agriculture was never particularly feudal; on the contrary it was very open to trade, by which it was stimulated. Although a rich agricultural society did exist, it was not peasant based, as the urban orientation of the ruling classes who profited from it testifies; the Arab world, centred in the courts of the soldiers, the clerics and the merchants of Baghdad, Basra or Aleppo, always presented a strong contrast to the Europe of the Manor Houses.

A lingua franca had long been prevalent in the area. Even before the Islamic invasions the region was unified by Aramaic. This Semitic language was to be replaced by Arabic without any great difficulties. In the following centuries linguistic unity was and continues to be practically total, if one does not count as separate languages the various regional ways of speaking which are distinguishable from one another only by accent and a few idiomatic expressions.

The countrysides stayed isolated from each other for twelve centuries and played no important political roles, even where they were reasonably prosperous for three or four centuries, as in Iraq. They resisted all attempts by the imperial power to dominate them, and their resistance was both military and religious. In the Mashreq the only really rural regions were all irredentist in religious terms — the mountains of Lebanon, shared between Maronite Christians and Shiite Moslems, the Alid Djebel and the Druse Djebel in Syria, or entirely Shiite Lower Iraq. The Shiite heresy furthered the development of a critical and even egalitarian spirit amongst these mountain peoples, a spirit to which official Sunnism was less favourable. During the Quarmate revolt the ideology of the insurgent slave-peasants of Lower Iraq was very similar. However, this does not mean that one can talk about feudalism here. At most only semi-feudal forms developed, during the periods of decadence of the great trade, and only in the plains which were more easily dominated by the townsmen and which could thus compensate, by a surplus expropriated from the peasants, for the fall in profitability of long distance trade. The plains of the Bekaa, of Palestine, of Homs, of Hama and of Middle Iraq were thus sometimes dominated by greedy landlords, particularly during the Ottoman period from 1500 onwards, during a long era of commercial decadence. Much later, from the 1930's onwards, modern use of agricultural land and the spread of irrigation techniques brought more and more land into the latifundia system.

The essential feature, however, was the towns. The towns were enormous; and when trade declined they were monstrous. Aleppo, Damascus, Baghdad, Basra and Antioch had several hundred thousand inhabitants and were among the most populated cities of Antiquity, of the Middle Ages, and of modern times till the advent of capitalism. They were far greater than anything in the West. At their height they held the majority of the area's population, which exceeded 5 million people; more people than at the beginning of the 20th century.

These towns have always been centres for courts, for merchants, and around them, for artisans and clerks, rather like the mediaeval Italian cities or those of the Hanseatic League. The accumulation of money wealth was the counterpart to the brilliance of the civilisation. In this urban and mercantile, but non-capitalist, civilisation such economic categories as money, merchant exchange and even wage-labour could be found. The cities of the Mashreq made up little rival worlds, the outlet for their advanced craftmanship being the long distance trade ventures of their merchants. The cultural unity of this dominant urban world was very pronounced: the towns were the centres of Arabo-Islamic culture, the citadels of Sunni orthodoxy.

The Maghreb

The same structures were to be found at the other end of the Arab world, in the Maghreb. Nomads and farmers had since time immemorial disputed a narrow territory, fenced in by the sea, the mountains and the desert. The *Pax Romana*, by building a series of fortified outposts all along the *limes*, pushed the Berber farmers southwards, to the detriment of Berber nomads and semi-nomads. Even before the arrival of the Arabs, the decadence of the Empire had allowed the nomads to spread out again, at the expense of the farmers. As for the Arabs, they avoided the mountainous strongholds of the peasants and built cities, which, as in the East, only survived and prospered thanks to the important long distance trade. This provided resources which it would have been far too difficult to draw from the exploitation of the farmers. The search for resources pushed the Arabs further and further, beyond the Mediterranean and the Sahara. To the South they met the great Berber nomads who shared their interests and sought to become the caravaneers of a flourishing trade. These nomads were to become Arabised much more quickly than the peasants. Ibn Khaldoun, an amazing scientific thinker and in some ways the founder of social science, was able to analyse the nature of these formations based on the profits of the great trade. All the great states of the Maghreb were based on the gold trade. For centuries, until the discovery of America, West Africa was the main source of gold for the whole of the Western Old World: for the Roman Empire, then for mediaeval Europe, and for the Ancient, then Arab, East. The gold trade crossed the desert, linking the Almoravid and Almohad states to the North, with the states of Ghana, Mali and Songhai to the South. The structures of these social formations were identical. Ibn Khaldoun and the Arab travellers of the period (Ibn Batouta, for example) were quite right to assimilate them all to the same model.

The nomad-town alliance and the exclusion of the peasantry from the civilised state were as much essential characteristics of the Maghreb as they were of the fertile crescent. French colonial ideologues have sought to analyse these structures in terms of racial opposition — Berbers (peasants) versus Arabs (nomads) — and to explain the decadence of the Maghreb by the ravages of the Arab nomads, cast as destroyers of agriculture and its works. Analogous hypotheses have been advanced concerning the Arab East: decadence would supposedly have been the result of destruction wrought by the nomads. In fact, however, the brilliant periods of Arab civilisation were not characterised by great agricultural achievements but, on the contrary, by the prosperity of the towns' trade and sometimes, associated with the prosperity of trade, by the ascendancy of great nomad tribes at the expense of the peasantry.

Decadence came with changes in the commercial routes. As these moved eastwards, there was a corresponding shift of the civilised states, both North and South of the Sahara. Thus, at first, we see the rise of the states of Morocco to the North, of Ghana and Mali to the South; later, as the gold trail moved towards Tunis, then Egypt, the Songhai and Haoussa states flourished in the South. Whilst in the Arab East the linguistically Arabised peasant strongholds attempted to preserve their autonomy by religious dissent, in the Maghreb it was by the maintenance of Berber language and culture that this desire for independence manifested itself.

Egypt

The history of Egypt is quite different. This oasis has nurtured one of the world's oldest peasant peoples. An enormous surplus could therefore be appropriated from the peasants by the ruling classes, thus providing the basis of civilisation.

State centralisation was here both precocious and extreme, made necessary by natural conditions — the need to organise huge irrigation works, and by military considerations — the need to defend the oasis against the menace of the nomads. To survive, Egypt fell back on itself, counting on sheer numbers to repel the enemy attacks. When Egypt conquered territories beyond the Nile Valley it was only in order to provide better defences for its peasant civilisation, by setting garrisons in the heart of the nomad and semi-nomad territory; to the East in Sinai and Syria, to the West in Libya. But, in Egypt itself, there never were, until the Hellenistic period, any real trading cities: the Pharaonic capitals were built on fields, in the middle of a densely populated countryside.

Egypt's traditional social formation was thus built on very different foundations from those of the East and the Maghreb. The peasant strongholds of the East and the Maghreb were autonomous and hardly integrated into the civilisation. Their level of development of the forces of production was generally very low, and on the whole they remained village-based communities. The Egyptian peasantry, on the other hand, abandoned this model over 4,000 years ago. In Egypt the dominant feature of the social formation was peasant-tributary not urban-mercantile. The peasants were not oppressed in groups, whilst holding on to the relative autonomy of a village community; they were oppressed individually, family by family. This tributary formation thus evolved of itself towards a type of feudalism similar to that of China, distinguished from Western feudalism only by its great centralisation, by the fact that the ruling class which appropriated the surplus was thoroughly organised into a state.

From the time of Alexander's invasion onwards, Egypt figures as a province of various empires based on the great trade: such was its role in the Hellenistic and Byzantine world, then in the Arab world. At the heights of these empires, when long distance trade flourished, an urban mercantile civilisation appeared. But the latter was always a foreign implantation, the product of the towns, merchants and courts. These towns only became really Egyptian with the decline of the long distance trade on which they had lived. This is as true of Hellenistic Alexandria as of Fostat and Cairo during the Arab period. The rural world of Egypt was not involved in these ups and downs: the only difference was that the surplus which it had once supplied to the Pharaonic ruling class was later handed over to foreign courts.

Nevertheless Egypt did become linguistically Arabised. But only when the Arab trading empire had begun to lose its *raison d'etre*. Indeed the slowness with which Egypt became Arabised had disastrous consequences: once the centre of civilisation, Egypt participated very little in the cultural, literary, philosophical and scientific blossoming of the first Arab centuries. The country was again forced to fall back upon itself, as the ruling classes became Egyptianised and more involved with the peasants. The latter gradually adopted Islam and Arabic, but several centuries passed before Coptic completely disappeared. Furthermore, even during Arabisation, the Egyptian people kept a very strong feeling of their own particularity. Far more than on the linguistic level — spoken Egyptian Arabic is only distinguishable from that of the East by accent — it was on the cultural level, and in its values, which remained peasant values, that Egypt maintained its originality.

The history of Egypt during the twelve centuries between the Arab conquest and Bonaparte's expedition can only be grasped if one understands the unfolding dialectic between its permanent peasant base and the occasional integration of the country into a much larger economic whole. During the three first centuries of its Arabisation, Egypt, merely the province of commercial empires based elsewhere, gradually lost its old personality without gaining a brilliant position in the new world to which it would from then on belong. Arab literature and sciences developed elsewhere; Egypt's contribution during these first centuries was lacklustre. The following six centuries, those of the Tulunid, Fatimid, Ayubid and Mameluk states, from the 10th to the 16th century were more favourable. The Turco-Mongol invasions weakened the Maghreb and undermined its commercial position. Egypt, having regained her independence, benefited by taking control of a new trade route which passed further south, through the Red Sea. The profits of this trade went to supplement the permanent wealth of the countryside. In turn these profits reinforced Egyptian urbanisation and stimulated agricultural production. These were the great centuries of Arabic literature in Egypt. In the important towns, wage labour and the various categories of mercantilism developed. Then came the Ottoman conquest. Egypt lost its hold on the long distance trade. Europe had definitely bypassed the Arab world and established direct naval links with Southern and Eastern Asia. The consequent decadence of the Egyptian cities rebounded on the countryside; the impoverished state could not maintain the irrigation system, and the ruling classes attempted to keep up their level of wealth by increasing the exploitation of the peasants. But, whatever the level of decadence of these three Ottoman centuries, Egypt, thanks to the permanence of its rural substrata, never fell to the same level of misery as Iraq, Syria and the Maghreb.

The fact that we stress the originality of each of these countries should not be taken as a denial of Arab nationalism. Regional particularities, enriching in themselves, remind one on the contrary of the roots of that nationalism — and imperialism further reinforces the profound tendencies towards unity.

The Peripheral Areas

To the South of Egypt, the Sudan belongs both to Black Africa and to the Arab world. In its Northern regions, Arab nomad tribes from the East, from the shores of the Red Sea, mixed with the original black populations to produce a nomadic pastoral civilisation. Furthermore these nomads — not only Islamised but Arabised on the linguistic level — fulfilled an inter-mediary commercial role between Egypt and the countries to her South. The central areas of the Sudan, on the other hand, kept their traditional agrarian civilisation, based on the clan-village community which is common to all Black Africa. These black peoples also eventually adopted the Arabic language, probably because of the long and thoroughgoing domin-ation exercised over them by the Arab nomads of the North. In the 19th century the Egyptian conquests of Mohammed Ali (1816-1848) and those of the Khedives who succeeded him until the British occupation (1882) and the revolt of the Mahdi (1882-1898) added to this domination that of the Egyptian military bureaucracy. But the Arabised black peasants have kept to this day their autonomous form of village organisation, a form now forgotten in Egypt. It was only much later, in certain areas developed by the British, notably the Gezireh, that a genuine agrarian capitalism appeared, to the profit of the nomad chieftains to whom the colonial power distributed the newly irrigated lands, thereby forcing the peasants into the proletariat. In other words we see here the same process as that which took place in Iraq at the time, during the period of the British Mandate; a process which engendered an agrarian capitalist economy equally foreign to both African and Arab tradition.

The South of the Arabian peninsula makes up a group of social for-mations which belong firmly to the Arab tradition. Agriculture never played a key role in the development of this civilisation; except in the Yemeni uplands, where the monsoon rains enabled a peasant community to survive, the civilisation of the area was exclusively urban and mercantile. The maritime empire of Mascate-Zanzibar typifies this perfectly, drawing its resources from its role as an intermediary between the Mediterranean world, black East Africa and India. Surrounded by nomads allied to the sea-going merchants, the Yemenite peasants, like those of the fertile crescent, maintained a relative autonomy by religious opposition; like the

Alids of Syria they are Shiites.

THE DOMINANT CHARACTERISTICS OF THE PRE-COLONIAL ARAB WORLD

Such was the pre-colonial Arab world: a whole stamped by its merchant character, with Egypt the only peasant exception. The ruling class of this world was urban, made up of courtiers, of clerics, of the little world of small artisans and clerks typical of Oriental cities. The ruling class was the cement which held things together: everywhere it had adopted the same language, the same orthodox Sunni Islamic culture. It was highly mobile, as at home in Tangiers as in Damascus. This was the class which made the Arab civilisation. Its prosperity was linked to that of the long distance trade. The latter was the basis for this class's alliance with the nomad tribes (its caravaneers) and for the isolation of the agricultural areas, which retained a distinct personality — linguistically (Berber) or in religion (Shiite) — but which did not play an important role in the system. Except in Egypt, the peasantry was only occasionally forced to supply tribute and even then, by the nature of things, the surplus expropriated was not large.

This Arab world was thus simultaneously diverse and deeply unified by its ruling class. It was in no way comparable to mediaeval feudal Europe, which was essentially a peasant culture. No doubt this explains why Europe was to evolve towards the constitution of separate nations: the European ruling classes, living off the surplus expropriated from the peasantry were forced to accentuate the diversity of the peoples. But that which made the unity of the Arab world possible was also the reason for its fragility: it was enough that the long distance trade declined for the towns based on it, and their states, to perish — leaving the misery of a world of nomads and small isolated peasant communities to highlight its decadence. This is what happened when the trade routes of Europe, Black Africa and the Far East no longer passed through the Arab world, when the sailors of the European Atlantic learnt to bypass it. Within this fragile whole, only Egypt survived: its high population density and its peasant character gave it a strong unity. One can talk of an Egyptian nation throughout history; the same can hardly be said of the Arab nation.

At the dawn of the imperialist aggression, during the 19th century, the decline of trade had put an end to the old unity of the Arab world. The Arab world had become no more than a heterogeneous conglomerate, under a foreign power, the Ottoman Empire. Imperialism was both to accentuate the divisions in this world and to bring about a rebirth of its unity.

The frontiers of the Arab world were those of merchant formations reliant upon the nomads. Wherever they entered a peasant country the Arabs, except in Egypt, were unable to set their mark upon the people.

This is the explanation of the Arab failure in Spain. The Arab merchant class remained urban, whilst the countryside was Christian. The Arabs, once expelled from Spain, left only monuments behind. Similarly the Turks were to fail in the Balkans. To reduce the Arab world to a feudal world analogous to that of Mediaeval Europe is the source of many serious mistakes, both on the political level and on that of the analysis of the national phenomenon in this part of the world.

The thesis formulated here flies in the face of so many opinions that we must make sure that it is firmly anchored. We must be sure that the following points are valid: firstly, that on the whole, the productivity of agriculture was mediocre and generally stagnant in the Arab zone, as opposed to its condition in Mediaeval Europe; secondly, that there was an overlap of the periods of brilliant civilisation with those of flourishing trade; thirdly, that the wealth of the civilisation in its brilliant periods was due more to the surplus drawn from trade than to that drawn from the local exploitation of the peasantry; and fourthly, that progress in agriculture, limited in time and space, was more the effect than the cause of the flourishing of commerce, that is to say that agricultural improvements were more extensive (extension of cultivated or irrigated areas, and population growth) than intensive (increases in productivity).

This is not all. Facts never speak for themselves, for they are always chosen and only shed light thanks to theoretical conceptions. The latter are, of course, drawn from observations and in their turn either allow us to situate events better, to have a clearer understanding of their movement, or must be revised. Four sets of questions are raised here: firstly, the question of knowing whether the common and dominant elements of this history are sufficient for us to be able to talk of a millenium of Arab history *in general*, despite variations in time and space; in other words does Arab unity have historical foundations and if so, which; secondly, the question of the origin and nature of the state, of the modes of agrarian production and of exploitation of the peasantry (feudal, tributary or some other mode of production), in other words the question of the origin and nature of the surplus and, concomitantly, of the structure of class exploitation in the area; thirdly, the question of the nature of the internal and external merchant relations, of their relative and absolute importance and of their articulation with the exploitation of direct producers, peasants, artisans and others, in other words the question of the nature of this so-called merchant formation (or set of formations) and the question of the field of its particularities (whether the latter appear only on the ideological and cultural level, or on that of the structure of state power, or even on that of the economic base — which raises the question of the internal and external circulation of the surplus); and fourthly, the question of the laws of this social formation's evolution, in other words the question of why it did not lead up to a capitalist development.

We will attempt to answer these questions when we draw the conclusions from our analysis and our propositions, in Chapter 5. But for the moment we feel that this broadly sketched picture of the past sheds light on our contemporary society on two levels.

The first level is that of the character of the transmitted ideology. Right from the beginning, the Islamic ideology translated the dominant character of the merchant relations for all the social formations which Islam was to affect in the Arab world. Not only is Islamic law a commercial rather than a peasant legal system, but it occupies a significant place in the religion. If this feature has spread out from its region of origin, it is because the Muslim state offered conditions very favourable to the blossoming of merchant relations. It is this same feature which explains why it was always merchants who introduced Islam to new areas, from Black Africa to Indonesia.

The second level is that of the national question. For the role of the mechant relations allows us to understand the distant origins of Arab unity. Commercial expansion made it possible for the surplus to be concentrated, whilst in feudal Europe it was scattered. When a social formation allows a ruling class concentrated in some very large towns to centralise and profit from a surplus generated by ten million peasants, the situation is very different from that in which the surplus (even if equal in volume per exploited peasant, which was not the case) is split up amongst rural lords each disposing of the fruits of the exploitation of only a thousand peasants. A chiefdom is not an empire. The centralisation of surplus and its circulation allows for the diversification of its forms, for wealth and civilisation. It gave an objective foundation to Arab unity. This unity was thus not the work of a feudal-rural aristocratic class but of a class of merchant-warriors. This is the foundation which underlies the persistence of the cultural and linguistic unity of the Arab zone, as opposed to the increasing differentiation of the European peoples and their gradual evolution into nations, nations which were to fully emerge as such only with the unification of the national capitalist markets.

Indeed Europe's backwardness — its feudal subdivision — was to be an important positive factor in the speed with which it later developed far more evolved relations of production, capitalist relations. The East, on the other hand, was handicapped by its advanced (tributary and non-feudal) relations of production and the merchant centralisation of the surplus. This essential thesis of 'unequal development' allows one to understand why Europe, because it was feudal, had to evolve both towards the formation of various nations, and towards the precocious emergence of capitalism, while the Arab world, because it was tributary and commercial, had to keep a more unified character despite the vicissitudes of history — and could not orient itself towards capitalism until it was integrated, by outside aggression, into the imperialist system dominated by Europe.

2

THE ERA OF IMPERIALISM (1880-1950)

The Arab world was quick to feel the threat which Europe represented. Even in the 16th century, during the age of mercantilism, the European merchants had been able to extract commercial privileges from the Ottoman authorities. The Arab merchant class was already defeated, Europe had won. For the following three centuries, the East slipped into a long slumber, and was quite unaware of what was going on in the West. The merchant-led growth of mercantile Europe had as its corollary the decrepitude of the Arab merchants' world. From then on the Arab cities decayed; the countryside, in all its heterogeneity, came to the fore again, and the very centres of any possible reflection on the decadence of the East ceased to exist. The awakening, at the dawn of the 19th century was to be a brutal one: Bonaparte's Egyptian campaign.

The history of the Arab's world long-lasting attempt at resistance was at first characterised by defeat after defeat: 1840 and 1882 for Egypt, 1830 and 1870 for Algeria, 1882 for Tunisia and 1911 for Morocco, 1919 for the Arab East. Then there was a period of renaissance, the growth of the anti-imperialist struggle, which still goes on,

The gradual integration of the Arab world into the capitalist system was thus initiated on a basis of inequality, even before that system became imperialist. For the first eighty years of the 19th century, Egypt desperately attempted to integrate itself as an autonomous participant in a new world. The first stage was marked by the efforts of Mohammed Ali, who started off a modernisation which was quite similar to that which the Meiji Restoration in Japan was to undertake half a century later. The khedives who succeeded him accepted the new international division of labour, but nevertheless sought to preserve Egypt's political independence. Algeria, conquered very early on by a still only semi-capitalist France, was to undergo a particular fate: it was profoundly marked by an attempt to radically destroy its personality, to assimilate it by turning it into a colonial settler state. With the rise of imperialism at the end of the century, the whole Arab world was definitely brought into the capitalist system as a dominated periphery. The regions which had already been integrated were remodelled by the new form taken by imperialist domination.

Before we examine the stages and modalities of this integration, the social transformations it involved, the reactions and political or cultural resistances it gave rise to, we must recall the fundamental theoretical theses which we apply to imperialism. These theses are particularly geared to understanding the development of capitalism at the periphery of its system, especially in terms of the transformation of agrarian modes of exploitation, the character of new social classes in the dominated countries, the stages in the unequal international division of labour and the role played in the world system by local bourgeoisies.

THE FUNDAMENTAL CHARACTERISTICS OF PERIPHERAL CAPITALIST SOCIAL FORMATIONS

The bourgeoisie and the proletariat are classes particular to the capitalist mode of production. They did not exist in pre-capitalist societies such as the Eastern pre-colonial Arab world. Therefore it is essential not to confuse the merchants of pre-capitalist systems with the commerical capitalists of the capitalist world.

At the centre of the capitalist system, the development of the capitalist mode has tended to destroy the old classes and to substitute the two new antagonistic classes, bourgeoisie and proletariat. A different pattern prevailed in the dominated periphery. There, the old modes of production — and hence the classes which correspond to them — were maintained. But these classes were transformed by imperialist domination, which subordinated the old modes to the capitalist mode. This meant that the general laws of capitalist accumulation dominated the whole system, that the surplus generated in the ancient modes was siphoned off, at least partially, by the dominant capital. It meant that the reproduction of the old modes was subordinated to the reproduction of capital. Furthermore, since the capitalist mode itself was introduced into these new peripheral capitalist formations, a local bourgeoisie and proletariat eventually emerged. This thesis implies that in the East the bourgeoisie's development was closely linked to its integration into the imperialist system. Essentially it was imperialist domination which engendered this new class, while limiting its expansion and directing it into particular sectors assigned to it by the international division of labour. It is therefore important not to confuse this new class with the old 'Third Estate' of the pre-imperialist mercantile Arab world, despite a certain link between them. Even more important, one must understand the dialectical contradiction in which this new class found itself: engendered by capitalism, its development was nonetheless limited by the latter.

The imperialist system itself has not remained static. On the whole, one can distinguish two phases of its development. In the first phase, imperialism denied the dominated countries any access to industrialisation; it pushed them into agricultural production and mining. The bourgeoisie of the dominated countries could therefore develop only in agriculture and in the sectors linked to integration into the world system (commerce, finance, transport, construction). In agriculture this produced a new class which we shall call the 'agrarian bourgeoisie'.

In the non-agricultural sectors the development of the bourgeoisie was, at this stage, strictly limited by the international division of labour. Apart from the commercial and financial intermediaries, the comprador bourgeoisie, there was hardly any bourgeoisie worth the name, since there were practically no industries. There was, however, the mere embryo of a bourgeoisie, drawn from a variety of sectors: commerce, transport, construction, the larger artisan enterprises, etc. This bourgeoisie soon came into conflict with imperialism, which denied it access to industry; it was still more of a potential bourgeoisie than an actual one. At this stage, because it came into conflict with imperialism, we can call it a national bourgeoisie. This bourgeoisie eventually imposed a revision of the international division of labour on imperialism. We then have the second phase of imperialism, dependent industrialisation on the import-substitution model. On this basis the bourgeoisie did develop, but it then lost its national character because its development was closely associated with the progress of imperialism.

Before we can talk meaningfully about a bourgeoisie, about bourgeois parties, we must situate these classes and organisations in time, in terms of the evolution of the imperialist system — and we must know which sections of the bourgeoisie we are talking about: those who profited from the international division of labour of a given period or those who struggled towards its revision. We must also be aware that, due to the extreme weakness of those sections of the bourgeoisie which struggled for a revision of the international division of labour, the bourgeois parties of the dominated East were unstable. The massive recruitment of petty-bourgeois elements which characterized them, and their extreme ideological confusion, bear this out. They were thus often reincorporated by those sections of the bourgeoisie which were quite satisfied with the status quo of the period.

Another characteristic stemming from this weakness is the role afforded to the bourgeois state. The state was eventually to fill the vacuum left by the inadequacies of a class which had on the whole remained a mere potentiality: thus we see Nasserist state capitalism arising out of a petty-bourgeois nationalist impulse.

Let us return to the transformations affecting the agricultural world, which was of paramount importance, both politically and socially, in the East. The integration of the Arab world into the capitalist system brought about a profound change: the evolution of the pre-capitalist agrarian structures towards agrarian capitalism. Similarly the new class of capitalist compradors was, by its very nature, in no way akin to the old class of non-capitalist merchants. These transformations demand further investigation.

The pure capitalist mode of production implies only two classes (bourgeois and proletarians) and two corresponding types of income (profit from capital and wages). A tributary mode of production (the feudal one, for example) implies two different classes (landowners and peasants) and corresponding incomes (ground-rent and peasant income). Different laws determine the production and distribution of the social product in each of these two systems. Profit presupposes capital, that is to say private appropriation of means of production — which are themselves the product of social labour; ground-rent, on the other hand, is the outcome of private appropriation of *natural* means of production, which are *not* products of social labour. Capital presupposes wage labour, i.e. free labour, a labour market and the sale of labour power. Ground-rent presupposes the bondage of a peasant worker, who is tied to the land not only by laws restricting his freedom but more generally by the simple fact that access to the natural means of production is controlled by others. Capital is essentially mobile and from this Marx deduces the transformation of value into prices of production, which guarantees an equalisation of profits on individual capitals; the appropriation of the natural means of production is essentially immobile and ground-rent varies from landholding to landholding. In the capitalist mode of production the transformation of value into prices of production masks exploitation, gives the illusion of a specific and autonomous productivity of capital, and thus constitutes the foundation of a specific form of ideology and of the alienation of the worker (alienation in the market). It thereby determines the specific relationships between ideology and the capitalist mode of production. Ground-rent is, on the contrary, a transparent phenomenon; it therefore presupposes that when the worker accepts the expropriation it represents, he does so from an ideological motivation very different from that of capitalism — in fact the ideological motivation is often a religious one. The tributary mode of production and its ideology therefore have a different relationship: here ideology is the dominant instance, while under capitalism the economic is not just dominant in the last instance, it is simply dominant. The capitalist mode of production therefore presupposes free access, by the capitalists, to the natural means of production; Marx insists on the non-capitalist character of ground-rent. However, the capitalist social formations did not develop out of nothing or in a vacuum. Capitalism grew in the bosom of previous formations, in new sectors not ruled by the relations specific to the previous modes of production. Later, when capitalism had come to dominate the formations as a whole, it spilled over into agriculture, where landed property became an obstacle to it. From then on the landlord (or his function) ceased to have a determinant role in agriculture, and made way for the capitalist farmer (whose function was, of course, often assumed by the landlord). In the advanced capitalist formations, there are no more landlords in the feudal pre-capitalist meaning of the word; there are only agrarian capitalists. The same is largely true in the Arab world today.

Marx's distinction between pre-capitalist landed property (feudal or peasant) was often to be lost sight of later. As early as 1858, Marx, in a letter dated 2nd of April, wrote to Engels that 'the modern form of landed property is the result of the action of capital on feudal landed property.' Marx had already analysed the transformation which had turned the English landlords into true agrarian capitalists. Physiocracy was the political economy of this transition, in which capitalism develops first in agriculture, until the industrial revolution allows it to expand into new sectors. Are these points only relevant to agriculture in the centre of the capitalist system? Not quite. Imperialist domination does, it is true, prevent capitalist transformation even in agriculture, the products of which are at first integrated only as merchandise. But this integration implies a process of subordination of the peripheral countries' agriculture to domination by capital, which brings about transformations of the same kind as those mentioned above.

In the Arab world, the old landlord class, where it existed (in Egypt), and the new classes of latifundist landlords established by imperialism (as in Iraq), underwent these transformations as a result of the integration of agricultural production into the capitalist market, to satisfy the demand for exports or (generally later) to meet internal needs. Although these classes sometimes hung on to the feudal bearing of the past, they were in fact increasingly subordinated to the laws of agrarian capitalism. For it was colonisation, and with it the development of a commerical agriculture (cotton in Egypt; vines, citrus fruits and olives in the Maghreb; cotton, wheat and dates in Iraq, Syria and Morocco, etc.) which reinforced, transformed and shaped, and sometimes simply created this class. Due to the pre-existence of non-capitalist relations of production in agriculture, the new agrarian bourgeoisie — latifundists or kulaks — had a complex appearance, half capitalist, half pre-capitalist (a term which we prefer to half-feudal as it covers a wider range of pre-capitalist relations, for instance the patriarchal one). This new bourgeoisie was capitalist not simply because it produced for the capitalist market but because this compelled it to adopt the behaviour which capitalist competition demands: to invest, to borrow, to calculate, to have recourse, at least partially, to wage labour, etc. At the same time this bourgeoisie used, and sometimes reinforced, the pre-capitalist methods of exploitation characteristic of the preceding social relations. We will call this class the 'agrarian bourgeoisie', to show that its main characteristic, the one on the rise, was capitalist. Thus this thesis is not just a matter of terminology, of substituting the term 'agrarian bourgeoisie' for 'feudalists'. It implies a change in the perspective of the analysis. The use of the terms 'feudalists' and 'bourgeoisie' to qualify a single industrial, commercial and financial bourgeoisie implies that one believes that this bourgeoisie is made up of two groups whose interests are in direct and irreconcilable opposition to one another. Our analysis, on the contrary, stresses that we are talking about a group which more and more formed a single fundamental class, and that, even if at first their interests were divergent, these interests tended to fuse in the very process of dependent development.

This process of transformation of the old land ownership system was more or less rapid according to the historical circumstances. It was slow in Egypt, a country which had strong landholding structures and where imperialist domination was forced to act through the political power of a local class ally (Egypt was not formally a colony; it was a protectorate only from 1914 to 1922, and the English occupation had no legal status). The class ally in question was the landholding aristocracy, which had been created by the khedives before the English occupation, and which had later called on the British to contain the national democratic movement. This aristocracy thus figured for a long time as an autonomous class, allied to imperialism and opposed to the (embryonic) national industrial bourgeoisie. This was the case from 1882 until the Thirties and Forties. The situation changed when the Misr group was forced to call in the capital of this aristocracy (and imperialist capital), in order to expand its interests in industry, and when the great agrarian holdings had become true capitalist operations in agriculture. From the Second World War onwards one can no longer speak of a national (industrial) bourgeoisie as opposed to the (supposedly feudal) landholding aristocracy: we are talking about a fusion between two sections of the same class. In other areas of the Arab world the landed aristocracy was directly established as such by imperialism during the Twenties: this happened in Iraq, in the Sudanese Gezireh, and in Morocco. Here the imperialist masters took the initiative of allocating the capitalist ownership of land to members of an old ruling class of a different kind (the traditional chieftains, who had never been landowners before), rather as the English did with the Zamindars in India.

There is a stubborn prejudice which holds that, in general, great landed property in the peripheral countries is a feudal vestige, whilst in fact it was sometimes purely and simply a creation of imperialist domination, and often the consequence of the integration of these countries' agriculture into the capitalist system: both the great Egyptian landholdings and the Turkish and Balkan *tchifliks* are examples. This prejudice probably stems from the fact that in China the landed aristocracy was originally pre-capitalist and stayed so, especially as the greater part of that enormous country was only very slightly integrated into the world capitalist system. But we should be wary of using a Chinese vocabulary (feudalists, bureaucratic bourgeoisie allied to and coming from the feudal class, pro-imperialist comprador bourgeoisie and national bourgeoisie) for other areas of the Third World.

Our conclusions on feudalism in the Arab world are thus as follows. First, during the pre-colonial eras the tributary mode of production was relatively undeveloped in the Arab world (with the exception of Egypt) and surplus was in the form of weak ground-rent; the main characteristic of the Arab formations of the great period was long distance trade, which permitted the transfer of surplus from other societies towards the Arab world. Secondly, the decline of long distance trade led to the appearance of a tributary feudal mode of production (with a high level of poverty) in the decadent Arab formations. Third, the economic development of the colonial period was primarily to the advantage of the landowners. Fourth, these landowners tended to become agrarian capitalists, and the pre-capitalist relations of domination and exploitation either gave way before the demands of capitalist competition, or were subordinated wholesale to domination by the laws of capitalism.

Imperialism thus allied itself with an old ruling class in order to install itself. But this alliance opened a new chapter of history, during which this old class progressively became a dependent bourgeoisie, as a result of the country's integration into the capitalist system.

THE NAHDA, LAST ATTEMPT AT RESISTANCE IN THE 19th CENTURY

The 19th century Arab renaissance, the *Nahda*, was centred mainly in Egypt and Syria. Already in the 18th century, Egypt, with Ali Bey, had attempted a first modernisation of the state, which presupposed its liberation from Ottoman rule. The circumstances following on Bonaparte's expedition led to a second attempt, that of Pacha Mohamed Ali. The Pacha's military bureaucracy — mostly Turks, Albanians and Circassians — became a ruling class which drew its resources from a peasantry made up of smallholding families. This surplus was used by the state to finance modernisation, irrigation works and the creation of a national army and industry. However, the Anglo-Turkish coalition of 1840 put a halt to this attempt at industrial renaissance.

No one can say what Egypt might have become without this European intervention. The analogy with Japan springs immediately to mind, and not without reason. The material progress achieved during the first forty years of the century was prodigious. Egypt had launched a process of modern industrialisation and economic diversification. The state workshops and manufactories employed hundreds of thousands of workers, they produced more cotton goods than most European countries, worked iron, produced steam engines and cannons, etc. All this was achieved with exclusively indigenous national managers in national industries.

The technology was imported, it is true; but it was quickly assimilated by young Egyptians who had been sent to France to learn the secrets of European science and technology. Much has been made of the obstacles which might have appeared at a later stage of this process (had it continued), of the autocratic character of the methods used by the Pacha to overcome any resistance, and of the superficial character of this modernisation, which did not reach people's 'souls'. The Pacha's project did not meet a very favourable response amongst the ruling class itself and the fact that he often relied on certain particular abilities (those of some merchant manufacturers for instance) and on adventurers and *parvenus* was often not well received. But the actions of both Peter the Great and of the Meiji had much the same characteristics and encountered the same difficulties. It is quite conceivable that Egypt could have become an autonomous capitalist power.[1]

Without considering this first grandiose and tragic attempt, one cannot understand either the nature of the eventual *Nahda*, nor the attempt, led by Orabi, at resistance to the English occupation.

The Pacha's successors, from 1848 to 1882, abandoned this autonomous direction, hoping, like Khedive Ismail, to Europeanise and modernise with the help of European capital, by integrating into the world market through cotton growing and by calling on European banking houses to finance this extraverted development. Within this framework, the Egyptian ruling class was to change its structure, to seize ownership of lands with the help of the state and to transform itself from a mandarin-type bureaucracy into a latifundist class. The country having already been turned into a cotton farm for Lancashire, the ruling class was quick to submit to the eventual English occupation, after obtaining guarantees that its privileges would be maintained. The English rewarded them handsomely, and this class was the main beneficiary of the enhancement of land values in the Nile Valley.

The urban 'Third Estate' (made up of clerks, artisans and the remains of the merchant world) and its rural equivalent (the village notables) reacted differently. As heirs to the cultural tradition, they were very much aware of the dangers colonisation presented to Arab and Egyptian civilisation. They were also aware of the harmful effects of imported merchandise. They therefore rejected European domination, and, having been let down by the Khedives and the Turco-Circassian aristocracy, were forced to rethink the whole issue of national survival. In Egypt, this Third Estate was the mainstay of the renaissance from 1880 onwards. But its attempt was to end in defeat, despite some impressive successes: a linguistic renaissance, a remarkable adaptation to the necessities of cultural and technical renewal, and a reawakening of the critical spirit. Faced with the imperialist menace, the aristocracy, out of self-interest and also because of their own Turkish origins, had rejected the traditions wholesale, although without achieving any counterbalancing real assimilation of European culture. The 'Third Estate', on the other hand, clung desperately to the traditions, in order to save its personality. At the same time its thinkers were fascinated by the power of the foreign enemy, and this brought about a critical re-evaluation of the traditions. In the short period which history granted them, between the time when the danger from outside was first perceived (1840) and the moment it materialised in the Occupation of Egypt (1882), the thinkers of the Third Estate were not able to overcome this contradiction between their desire to preserve their own individual characteristics and their will to catch up with Europe. In the end, they drove up a blind alley: the empty affirmation of a local character and personality which was to lead to that neurotic loyalty to tradition which paralyses movement. This was the manifestation, on the ideological level, of the emerging bourgeoisie's powerlessness against the imperialist threat, of its inability to really develop on capitalist lines.

On the political level this Third Estate effectively did attempt to reject integration into the emerging imperialist system, an integration which was accepted — solicited even — by the old bureaucratic ruling class which had become first a landholding aristocracy then an agrarian bourgeoisie; the course chosen by this latter class led necessarily to the national betrayal which came to fruition in 1882. In this sense the national and patriotic struggle led by Ahmad Orabi can be called bourgeois and anti-imperialist. We must remember, however, that the Egyptian bourgeoisie was then still very much in embryo, still stuck in the pre-capitalist past. It was made up more of merchants, artisans, small manufacturers, administrators and intellectuals than of capitalist industrialists. Mohamed Ali's attempt at transformation had not lasted long enough to create a bourgeoisie in the full sense of the word. It was precisely because of the difficulties encountered in the formation of such a bourgeoisie that the Pacha had established a state economic system, a system which had been entirely dismantled as from 1840, by order of the English — and in the name of free enterprise.

Several nuances must be introduced into the analysis of this Egyptian *Nahda*. They reflect the composite character of the 19th century Egyptian bourgeoisie, which is why we prefer the term 'Third Estate'. The brothers Selim and Bichara Takla, who founded Al Ahram in 1876, were not true representatives of the levantine comprador bourgeoisie: the newspaper's Egyptian, Ottoman and pro-French (not to say anti-English) line bears this out. Throughout the period there were intermediaries between the openly collaborating landholding aristocracy and the nationalist current. For before accepting imperialist rule the Egyptian ruling class had attempted to put up some resistance, by modernisation of the country 'from above', even after 1840. In this context one can understand why a man like Tahtawi could participate in such a task. During half a century, from 1820 to 1870, Tahtawi sought to integrate the contribution of idealist European bourgeois nationalism into a renovated Arab culture, and to this end accepted political responsibilities under Mohamed Ali and those of his successors who opted for modernisation of Egypt. Defeat finally discouraged Tahtawi: the balance of power, too strongly weighted against Egypt, underlined the contradictions of a movement which sought to guarantee the independence and national character of a country whilst admitting to the advantages of Europeanisation.

Syria was the other pole of this 19th century renaissance. Syria's Mediterranean position explains its early understanding of the imperialist danger. But the economy of the Mashreq countries, still firmly tied to the Ottoman Empire, was stagnant. Set apart from both the old commercial circuits and the new current of colonisation to which Egypt was opening up with the cotton industry, the Syrian towns were deprived of their once brilliant elite. Thus, as in Egypt, the renaissance was fueled by the semi-popular elements of the Third Estate: artisans, clerics and clerks. The economic and social misery of Syrian life at the time, however, limited the influence of the *Nahda* there.[2] *Mutatis mutandis*, what Marx had seen in the Germany of his time took place: the misery of real social life displaced the locus of struggle from the political field to the field of ideas alone. The Eastern *Nahda* began in the modernised schools of Lebanon as early as 1820-1830, then spread to Syria, where Nasif Yazeji and Boutros Boustani founded a Syrian Scientific Society in 1857, to carry out the same task of spiritual modernisation as was being attempted in Egypt. But the Syrian *Nahda* went no further. For lack of an adequate class base, the movement failed to transcend the opportunistic hopefulness which characterised it especially after the fall of the despotic sultan, Abdul Hamid, in 1909, and the success of the Young Turks. The Ottoman party of decentralisation achieved nothing. The most far-seeing elements — Abdel Rahman Kawakebi and Najib Azouri — were forced into exile, where in 1904 they founded the League of the Arab Nation, based in Paris. The weakness of the *Nahda* explains the fact the during the 1914-1918 War, the Arab nationalists saw no alternative to an alliance with the Allies.

Although the Egypto-Syrian *Nahda* did not manage to formulate a coherent and efficacious programme of social transformations, as would have been necessary to resist the imperialist aggression, it was nonetheless a decisive factor in the formation of modern Arab feeling. For it re-established the flow of ideas between the provinces of the Arab world, and uniformly remodelled the language by adapting it to the common need for modernisation — in short it revivified the main instrument of Arab unity.

THE WITHDRAWAL INTO PROVINCIALISM

After the failure of the *Nahda* came a darker period, characterised by a withdrawal into provincialism which lasted until the Second World War. This was the period of imperialism triumphant; it was also the period of defeat for the bourgeois nationalist movement, which had to fall back on provincial strongholds. Finally, this was the period of Zionist settlement in Palestine.

During the century of history we have been talking about, two features appeared and developed everywhere in the Arab world, sharply in some places, more slowly in others. Firstly, the Arab renaissance saw the rise of a new class, the urban petty bourgeoisie spawned by the Arab world's integration into the imperialist sphere. This class was eventually to take over both from the old ruling class which was rapidly falling apart, and from the new bourgeois class called forth by the world system. Secondly, this renaissance was translated into a growing awareness of Arab unity. Precisely because the Arab world (excepting Egypt) had never been a peasant world, and because the renaissance could not base itself on authentic national peasant cultures, its vehicle, the urban bourgeoisie, sought to revive the Arab unity of old: that of language and culture. In places such as Egypt, where on the contrary the renaissance could base itself on the unity of the national peasantry, the feeling of Arab unity could not find its expression as easily; this furthered a rebirth of national feeling.

Egypt was the first province of the Arab world to react to the foreign danger. But it was the Israeli menace which was later to make it quite clear that Egypt's fate was that of the Arab world as a whole. As for the Arab East, its awakening had to wait until imperialism had actually installed itself in the heart of the area and had laid down the foundations of the future State of Israel. Right from the start, therefore, the anti-imperialist struggle was intertwined with the struggle against Zionism. The Maghreb, isolated and colonised by another power, France, only became aware of the problems of Arab unity in 1967. Thus, little by little, the Palestinian problem became the pivot of the Arab question, the test of the ability of the various social classes which had pretensions to lead the national anti-imperialist movement. This was the test which broke first the comprador bourgeois and latifundist generation, then the socialist petty bourgeoisie.

One cannot avoid the fact that the emergence of modern pan-Arab feeling was gradual and belated. There was too much regionalism in the decadent Arab world of the 19th century for it to be otherwise. This does not mean that, when faced with Europe's imperialism, the various Arab peoples did not feel the need to unite and to overcome these regionalisms. One should not overlook the community of language, of culture, and, to a great extent, of religion. Mohamed Ali had been aware of both the danger from Europe and the need to break away from the decrepit rule of the Ottomans — and he had realized that to do so, Egypt, Syria and Arabia had to be united by a common effort. But he was defeated. Closer to our time, during the First World War, a new and lively pan-Arabism appeared in Egypt and in the Mashreq. And throughout the French occupation of the Maghreb, the links between the nationalists of the Maghreb and the Arab East were never broken. Even before the Algerian War and the sheltering of the F.L.N. in Cairo, the religious university of El Azhar had welcomed thousands of Maghrebians who had refused Francization. But one must admit that pan-Arabist feeling could, at this stage, be manipulated by imperialism and by the social classes which kept the ball of domination rolling in the semi-dependent states between the wars. Great Britain, which had been behind the Arab revolt in 1916, was still to be found pulling strings backstage during the 1945 Alexandria Conference which gave birth to the Arab League. These same reactionary forces were quite capable, when the need arose, of playing on local specificities to justify their withdrawal into provincialism.

Egypt

The military defeat of Orabi, in 1882, put an end to the hopes of the *Nahda*. The Third Estate was liquidated, first politically, then economically. The generation of petty bureaucrats which replaced it was quick to accept foreign domination, and took refuge in a refusal of modern values, in a reactionary and riskless opposition. Naturally there were brilliant exceptions to this rule, such as Mustapha Kamel, Mohammad Farid and Loufti el Sayed. Furthermore, when really intense struggle was going on, the petty bourgeoisie was sometimes able to commit itself as a whole, and to give a better account of itself.

At the same time, within the structure of colonial rural improvements, a real Egyptian bourgeoisie began to grow; agrarian at first, it then became agro-capitalist, and even industrial. The landholding aristocracy, which had gradually become capitalist, launched itself from 1919 onwards into commercial and industrial business. The Misr group was formed, and eventually operated as an associate of the main foreign capitals — those of Egypt's levantine bourgeoisie (Greeks, Europeanised Jews, Europeanised Eastern Christians, etc.) and those of British, French and Belgian capitalism. This class thus became the Egyptian ruling class, the transmission belt of imperialist domination until 1952. The Misr group, for example, was originally constituted as an industrial and banking capitalist group which sought to be independent of the landed aristocracy and imperialism. But it was immediately faced with ten years of frustration. Little by little it had to submit to a hard reality — and to call in the financial resources of the levantine compradors, of imperialism and of the great landowners, in order to develop.

After the abortion of the 19th century renaissance, Egyptian society ceased to think for itself. The aristocracy, and the bourgeoisie which grew out of it, were content with a European veneer; the petty bourgeoisie concentrated on coffee house gossip; the proletariat hardly existed; and the disinherited masses of the people, increasingly numerous, were dehumanised and reduced to the daily struggle for the piastre, for elementary survival. Colonial Egypt met all the conditions for the emergence, as a sort of reaction, of an intelligentsia, of a group of men who were forced to seek truth outside of a society into which they could not integrate because of its inadequate development. This was the context for Mustapha Kamel and Mohammad Farid's first Egyptian Nationalist Party, which endured from 1900 to the First World War. Created by men of the intelligentia's first generation, the first Nationalist Party was by no means the party of the Egyptian bourgeoisie: the Egyptian bourgeoisie of the period was an aristocracy with bourgeois tendencies which accepted foreign rule. Nor was this party that of the rural kulak bourgeoisie, which had its own organisation: the Umma Party, jealously conservative in all ideological and social matters and a faithful supporter of the efficient English administration, thereby proving that the rural middle classes of the period already felt some solidarity with the aristocracy in the face of the danger which the growing mass of landless peasants represented. The Nationalist Party was, however, a bourgeois party in the sense that its modern ideology drew on the European bourgeois tradition. Despite the misery of Egyptian society, despite the apathy of the impoverished masses, the inconsistency of the petty bourgeoisie, the reactionary attitude of the rural middle classes, despite the open treason of the aristocracy and of the bourgeoisie which had grown out of it, the Nationalist Party found many echoes. At critical moments the Party became the nation — whose potential it symbolized. But the Nationalist Party's history was to be short. At the very moment when the whole nation rose up in 1919, it disappeared to be replaced by a party which was more truly representative of Egyptian society at the time: the Wafd.

The formation of a bourgeoisie dominated by imperialism was contradictory in many ways. Firstly, because the Egyptian bourgeoisie was not homogeneous: the agrarian branch benefited from imperialist domination and therefore adopted an attitude analogous to that of the commercial compradores; the industrial branch which aspired to industrialisation was national but its material base was almost non-existent. Under these conditions the bourgeois parties could not escape the consequences of their predominantly petty bourgeois membership, of the weak lead from the bourgeoisie. Their ideology and their ambitions made them seem far more bourgeois than they actually were. Such was the case with the first Egyptian Nationalist Party. It fought against imperialism and even prepared the victory of 1919-1924, which resulted in independence on the political level, and the revision of the terms of the international division of labour on the economic level, with the beginnings of import substitution industry between the wars. But while it was the people and the petty bourgeoisie who fought, it was the latifundist and comprador bourgeoisie who profited, since only the latter could go into industry in association with imperialist capital. Let us examine how, on the basis of this economic substratum, political life evolved during 1919-1952, a period marked by the opposition between the Wafd and the King.

The Wafd, whose history dominates that of Egypt from 1919 to 1952, was also not the party of the Egyptian bourgeoisie. The main section of that bourgeoisie stayed fundamentally pro-monarchist and pro-British. The inconsistency of the Wafd was thus that of the petty bourgeoisie — which explains the fact that it showed itself to be as reactionary as the monarchist parties in all fundamental matters and that it never developed any programme of agrarian reform, for example. The English never took its nationalist demagogy seriously. The Wafd in no way envisaged the possibility that Egypt might cease to be a client state of Great Britain's. The British were very skilfully able to use the existence of a monarchy which openly accepted their presence to keep their concessions to the Wafd at a minimum. Whenever any real danger threatened the arrangement, the British quickly found the basis for a compromise, as in 1936 and 1942, when faced with the fascist menace. The Anglo-Egyptian Treaty of 1936 was to settle for 20 years the area of interest set aside for the English in Egypt: the negotiation of this treaty which had dragged on since 1924, was suddenly speeded up by the threat to Egypt from the year old Italian occupation in Ethiopia. The successive British concessions, and the rapid development of light industry from 1920 to 1945, made compromise easy. Thanks to this cohesion the system worked despite occasional crises: for 25 years the alternation of Wafdist parliaments and royalist dictatorships was enough to ensure the continuity of foreign and aristocratic interests.

The lull in economic growth, the tremendous numerical increase of the disinherited masses, who ended up representing 50% of the population in the towns and 80% in the countryside, as well as the flowering of the middle classes on the one hand, the appearance of communism on the political scene and the crisis of the colonial system in Asia on the other, brought about the post-war break-up. The period of harmonious economic development in the framework of the colonial system and successive compromises with Britain was drawing to an end.

Here too the Wafd suffered from the weakness of the Egyptian bourgeoisie where the latter had transcended the agrarian sector to become agro-comprador-monopolistic. Furthermore, secondary contradictions make it impossible to consider the agrarian bourgeois class as homogeneous, for it was made up of latifundists at one pole, and of kulaks at the other. The latter were certainly reactionary but were also aware that their own development was held back by the concentration of land ownership in the hands of the former. In the urban areas the weakness of the bourgeoisie in the sectors it did not monopolise caused a deformation in the role of petty bourgois recruitment to the organisation, giving it a significance which it did not have in the European bourgeois parties, for instance. Thus the contradictions specific to the petty bourgeoisie were to gain a certain autonomy in the life of the organisation. Furthermore the Wafd always had a radical democratic wing — although a patently weak one, which explains why the dominant sector of the bourgeoisie was always able to reintegrate the party in the end, and why the imperialists were able to limit the impact of the Wafdist opposition. The history of this party could quite probably have been different. If the radical wing had carried the day, the Wafd would have become the equivalent of the first Kuomintang under Sun Yat Sen, creating conditions favourable to the development of

democracy and autonomous action of the popular masses. It is because
the Wafd did not choose this path that it went bankrupt and thus paved
the way for Nasserism.

Throughout this whole long period during which Egypt fell back upon
itself, national feeling was strictly Egyptian; only the forms of imperialism
were challenged, in attempts to find compromises which would make it
more bearable. Nobody sought to place the Egyptian anti-imperialist
struggle in the larger context of the Arab world. Although the Palestinian
revolt of 1936 found many echoes, notably amongst the masses of the
people, there was no specific organisation or party through which these
feelings could be expressed. The only movements having the right to
speak were those of the collaborationist bourgeoisie or of the erratic and
non-rebellious petty bourgeoisie. And these groups were no longer rooted
in Egyptian history, since they were products of colonisation. Taha Husayn,
expressing an extreme ideological point of view which, while not necessarily
indicative of the general mood, was nevertheless significant, went so far as
to claim that Egypt owed nothing to the Orient, being a daughter of Greece
and Europe. A superficial Westernism came to hide a real cultural
emptiness — and allowed for a cheap self-satisfaction: 'Since we have never
been Orientals, we have always been the equals of the Westerners, who
have nothing to teach us.' These attitudes tied in nicely with the ways of
the aristocracy, and the defeat they represented was to be symbolised
twenty years later by the self-criticism of Taha Husayn, who went on to
sing the praises of the new regime's Arab traditionalism.

Nevertheless one cannot condemn Egyptian bourgeois thought of the
period wholesale. Its more advanced sections pursued the work of the
Nahda. For instance, one should not underestimate the proclamation made
in 1925 by Sheikh Ali Abdel Razek[3], which described the Caliphate as a
temporal institution having nothing to do with Islam. The abolition of the
Ottoman Caliphate by Mustapha Kemal, in 1924, had been a shock; it put
an end to a millenium of history during which the state and Islam had
always been intertwined. It meant that the modern era had definitely
arrived, the era of capitalism and later, of socialism. The state had to be
separated from religion — which was no easy thing to accept. If so many
Christians figured in the history of the *Nahda* in Egypt and in Syria, as in
the Wafd and the Arab left, it was because they could accept this theme of
the secular state far more easily than could their Muslim fellow-citizens.
The bourgeoisie as a whole no longer dared to take this step, having ceased
to be revolutionary and anti-imperialist; and the proletariat was not yet
expressing itself to any great extent. The importance of this proclamation
of secularity is highlighted when one considers that considerable sectors of
the petty bourgeoisie, for all the anti-imperialism of some of their attitudes,
refused to accept it. And one should be aware of how great a step back-
wards was the revival, twenty years later, of the Muslim ideology peddled
by the Muslim Brotherhood: *Islam and Social Justice*,[4] which was to have

important repercussions in the Fifties, maintained a diametrically
opposite point of view, as a response to the 'marxist challenge'. Of course,
as time went by, liberal bourgeois thought atrophied and ended up in a
rapid cosmopolitanism. There were soon only a few diehard veterans, such
as the Syrian, Sati Al Housri, to carry on an Arab nationalist dialogue
within the Arab League, a dialogue redolent of idealist European rational-
ism, which was no longer that of the bourgeoisie, and had not become that
of the petty bourgeoisie, far less that of the proletariat.

The Mashreq

The same provincialism characterised the political life of the Mashreq
during the period. But there, because the imperialist powers had shared
out the region amongst themselves as British and French Mandates, and
because Zionist settlement directly threatened the survival of the area, the
national reaction was more united and more Arab. Ottoman domination
of the fertile crescent had preserved the unity of the area until 1919. Of
course, this domination did not guarantee any effective protection against
imperialist penetration. The whole Ottoman Empire was heading towards
underdevelopment and indirect colonisation, since the capitulations had
granted exorbitant privileges to European capital and merchandise. The
destruction of maritime Syria, which goes back to the Crusades, had
allowed the Europeans, especially the Italian city-states, to dominate
sea-going Mediterranean trade. The opening of the Atlantic and Cape sea-
routes had deprived the fertile crescent of its active mercantile role. From
the 19th century, the development of European capitalism accelerated the
Arab East's process of degradation. The first half of the 19th century saw
the destruction of the Syrian artisans, as a consequence of the influx of
English cotton goods. Later, the penetration of European capital worked
through the Ottoman Debt which, in 1874, swallowed four-fifths of the
Turkish Government's budget. To cope with this pillage, Istanbul drew
more and more on the tributary exploitation of its dependent territories:
by the end of the 19th century more than 80% of the fiscal revenue drawn
from the Vilayets of Syria and Mesopotamia were handed over to the
Turkish Government as tribute; less than 20% being set aside for local
administrative expenditure. On top of all this there was the direct
penetration of European capital, although this did not amount to much
in 1914: a few industrial firms in Syria, railway and port management,
and the setting up of a few public services (electricity, water supply). The
major achievements (the Berlin-Baghdad line and the exploitation of the
Mossoul oil fields) were still at the project stage when the First World
War broke out. The integration of the fertile crescent into the world
capitalist system was thus much slower than that of Egypt or the Maghreb.
In fact, it only really began during the period of the Mandates. In Syria,
this integration remained feeble right up to the post-war period, mainly

because the area was unsuited for a developed export agriculture. Nevertheless, from the Fifties onwards, the Gezireh, a semi-arid steppe occupied till then only by nomadic shepherds, was developed for cultivation. The Syrian urban bourgeoisie used modern capitalist means to enhance the value of the land: tractors and a limited wage-earning work-force, large plots hired from the state or from the nomad chieftains. This made for a considerable increase in exports of cotton, wheat and barley. Characteristically for Syria, it was in an area with no real peasantry that progress in agricultural development took place. In the traditionally rural West, on the other hand, progress was hampered by the social organisation of the peasant world. For ever since Syria had lost its old commercial role a process of social regression had set in. The population had fallen, from 5 million inhabitants during the great periods of Antiquity and of the Abassid Caliphate,to less than a million and a half just before the First World War. Furthermore, this population was largely urban: in 1913 a third lived in the towns, a quarter were nomads and only 40% lived in the agricultural countryside.

The commercial role of the cities was minute, limited to the Arabic and Mesopotamian hinterland. The destruction of the artisan class by competition from European imports aggravated the crisis. It was then that, in order to survive, the Syrian urban ruling class became increasingly feudal, seeking to draw from the peasants of the Syrian West the surplus which trade no longer supplied. The setting up of latifundia started during this 19th century marked by a bourgeoisie deprived of its functions and forced to fall back on the countryside. Between the wars, under the Mandate, this feudalisation accelerated, thanks to the 'French peace' which made possible the exploitation of peasants who had until then been able to resist oppression. The urban bourgeoisie, to whom the domination of French capital denied a role in industrialisation, had no other choice. After Syrian independence, this bourgeoisie found a new lease of life in the setting up of light industries (textiles, food industries) and in the agricultural conquest of the Gezireh: 'Agricultural growth, an urban victory' wrote Rizkalla Hilan.[5] It was only in 1955 that this process ran out of steam and drew to an end, forcing Syria to start on a new path, that of state capitalism.

The Syrian case shows how, from 1920 to 1955, integration into the world capitalist system gave the local bourgeoisie the opportunity for some small development and how this integration shaped a client and dependent national bourgeoisie. The limited satisfaction afforded this bourgeoisie explains how and why Syria, the living centre of Arabism in 1919, could fall into 35 years of provincial slumber.

The same thing happened in Iraq. In 1920 the English moved into a semi-desert country, without any towns worth mentioning: even decadent Syria was considerably more developed. But the place had many natural possibilities. The English therefore set out to recreate an agricultural world which had disappeared centuries before: the irrigation works carried out under the Mandate were to play a decisive role in the constitution of a new latifundist agrarian bourgeoisie. The English distributed 90% of the lands to a thousand Sheikhs, chieftains of semi-nomadic tribes. Oil, exploited by the Iraq Petroleum Company, did the rest. This enhancement of value gave birth to an Iraq which, for all its turbulence, pan-Arabism and nationalism, remained a faithful British client state until 1958.

The urban world of the fertile crescent, miserable as it was towards the end of the Ottoman era, stayed resolutely nationalist and united. Faced with the threat of imperialism, it had long been pro-Ottoman; its nationalism then ran a zigzag course between 'Muslim', 'Ottoman' and 'Arab' nationalism. Eventually, disappointed by inadequate Ottoman reforms, notably by the 1829 Tanzimat, even more disappointed when from 1908 the Young Turk movement moved toward a Turkish and even anti-religious nationalism, the urban Arab world of the area turned towards Arab nationalism proper. Just before 1914 a Syrian, Jamil Mardam Bey, and an Iraqi, Hamdy al Pachachi, founded Al Fatat, the Young Arab movement. And Arab officers of the Ottoman Army formed the Al Ahd society, which included amongst its members Nuri Al Said, who was to be the liegeman of the English in Iraq for the next forty years.

It was then that the Arab nationalists sought out the external alliance which would enable them to throw off the Ottoman yoke. British diplomacy was quick to use them and to trick them. Hussein, Sheriff of Mecca, rose up against the Turks in 1916, proclaiming himself 'King of the Arabs' and his son, Faycal, was proclaimed constitutional monarch of independent Greater Syria (Syria and Palestine) in 1919, by the Syrian National Congress, called at Damascus by the urban Arab nationalists. But the great powers involved had other ideas: a secret Anglo-French agreement, the so-called Sykes-Picot Agreement, had already carved up the area into English and French colonies. The Arabs were immensely disappointed and they bitterly resented their submission to the demands of the victorious imperialist powers. It took the occupying armies several years to re-establish order. The English managed to divide this Arab nationalist movement by buying over its weakest element, the desert chieftains whom the bourgeoisie had thought fit to give itself as kings, thus renewing the traditional alliance between the merchant towns and the nomads. The desert lords — the Hashemite family — accepted the carve up and were rewarded by becoming the kinglets of British mandates: Faycal in Iraq and his brother Abdallah in Transjordan.

In Iraq, the slide into provincialism was helped along by the potential wealth of the country and by the enhancement of land values, as well as by the skilful tactics of the British. The reign of Faycal I (1921-1933) saw the end of the Arab nationalism of the Ottoman era. The three parties which sat in the Parliament were little more than cliques of satisfied notables who had done well out of the distribution of newly enhanced lands. Furthermore, Britain managed to sign an unequal treaty with Iraq in 1930, which granted Iraq the appearance of independence but in fact made it a client state. Although Iraq may seem to have then gone through a period of instability and volatile government coalitions, the two basic features of the status quo (socially, domination by the new latifundist class, and internationally, Iraq's client status) were not challenged by any of the regimes until 1958. However, the first new generation of the Arab nationalist opposition was forming during the Thirties. The intellectuals of the Ahali Group were no more the representatives of the bourgeoisie than was the Egyptian Wafd. In Iraq too the bourgeoisie was openly collaborationist. The milieu of the Ahali Group was quite simply a relatively isolated intelligentia; however it was from this group that the main political forces of the future were eventually to emerge. The milieu's main tendency — the socialist-tinged populism of Kamel el Jaderdji — organised itself into a party, the National Democratic Party, starting from 1943. After 1958, in the Kassem era, it was to play a decisive role. Further to the left, Abdel Fattah Ibrahim organised the National Unionist Party, which took a more resolutely pan-Arabist stance. Even further left, the milieu's most radical elements formed the Iraqi Communist Party during the Second World War. Other members of the Ahali Group, notably Sami Shawkat and Sediq Shonsol, were eventually to establish the Futuwwa tendency in 1939, the distant ancestor of the Baath. Before the War, However, these groups did not play any role comparable to that of the Wafd in Egypt, probably because the Iraqi latifundist bourgeoisie was on the whole quite satisfied with the advantages it drew from British colonisation.

One should not be misled by the many coup d'etats which took place in Iraq between 1936 and 1946. The first of these, organised by General Bakr Sidqi in 1936 during the reign of Ghazi I (1933-1939), brought a reformist from the Ahali Group Hikmat Sulaiman, to power. But, under pressure from the bourgeoisie, Hikmat Sulaiman abandoned his friends on the left wing of the Ahali Group, thereby paving the way for his own downfall and the assassination of General Sidqi in 1937. In fact, Hikmat Sulaiman, an admirer of Ataturk, thought in terms of reforms imposed from above without interfering with the privileges of the new latifundist bourgeoisie. Hence the mediocrity of the reforms, which amounted to little more than improvements in administration. Hikmat Sulaiman, who represented no consistent Iraqi social class, went so far as to attempt to direct Iraq away from the paths of Arabism: the Saadabad Pact, aimed against the Kurds, was signed in 1937 with Turkey, Iran and Afghanistan, right in the middle of the Arab revolt in Palestine.

The governments which followed the pro-Nazi coup d'etats of 1937 and 1941, leading up to that of Rachid el Gaylani in April 1941, were just as mediocre. Their whole enterprise was nothing but a petty internal quarrel within the ruling class, some cliques having come to the conclusion that the Axis powers might be more consistently generous with their crumbs than the British. The Regent, Abdullilah (Regent, 1939-1953), the faithful Nuri al Said and, in April 1941, the British Army, made short work of these paltry conspirators.

Iraq's withdrawal into provincialism was punctuated by the Hashemite monarchy's great display of pan-Arabist verbal demagogy. It was tempting for the Baghdad kinglets to play at being Abassid Califs, for all their real lack of power — and to contrast the achievements of Hashemite Iraq (its formal independence) with the status of Syria, Palestine or Egypt. In fact nothing resulted from this parody of pan-Arabism: when, in 1936, Iraqi volunteers led by Fauzi Kaukji went to help the Palestinian insurgents, the Hashemite monarchy did nothing more than offer its hospitality to the rather shady Mufti of Jerusalem and bring into the Government the even more shady Rashid Ali.

Things carried on like this until 1958. First Regent Abdullilah, then Faycal II (1953-1958) and Nuri el Said clashed more and more violently with the Iraqi people in 1948, when they attempted to impose on the country the renewal of the British Protectorate (the abortive Portsmouth Treaty); then again in 1952 with the renewal of the Iraq Petroleum Company's concession; and finally in 1955, when they imposed on Iraq the anti-Soviet Baghdad Pact. The treachery of the bourgeoisie had, even in the Thirties, moved the patriotic intellectuals of the Ahali Group more and more to the left, towards Marxism or populism. The workers in the oil industries of Mossoul and Kirkouk, the dockers of Basra, the urban world of artisans, wage earners and state employees, the world of the petty bourgeoisie and that of the peasants and nomads all provided a receptive popular audience for this radicalism. Its success in the towns was rapid. The Iraqi Communist Party, which had been born out of this leftward drift of the Ahali Group, was still hesitating, in 1958 and even afterwards, between two political lines: between a proletarian line and a petty bourgeois line. To stress the former line in no way led away from the goal of national liberation (liberation of Iraq and of the whole of the Arab East, since the two were necessary to each other); but it did mean understanding that, given the conditions of the period, this task could not be accomplished under the leadership of the latifundist bourgeoisie. It meant grasping that the task could only be carried out by the proletarianised and semi-proletarianised masses of the towns and countryside under the ideological leadership of the proletariat. Under Yusuf Salman Yusuf ('Fahd', assassinated in 1949 by the King's police) the Communist Party did choose this revolutionary line, with the dual consequence that it enjoyed some considerable success amongst the popular masses in the towns, and that its right-wing elements split off to form a fraction around Daud Sayegh in 1943. Such splits continued throughout the difficult years between 1949 and 1955, after the assassination of the revolutionary leadership, and then after 1958, during the Kassem regime. The populists, even more than the rightist communists, were most successful amongst the masses of the petty bourgeoisie. The left wing of this populism found its expression in Jaderdji's National Democratic Party, in the groups which flirted with the rightist communists, in Abdel Fattah Ibrahim's National Union, and in the 'Partisans of Peace' led by Aziz Cherif during the Fifties. But there was a right wing to this populism, which was frightened by the threat of revolutionary dynamism inherent in the leftist communists. This right wing had come out of the pre-war Futawwa movement and had supported Rashid Ali's pro-Nazi regime. It reorganised itself from 1949 onwards with the advent of the Islah (reform) movement, fused with Salih Jaber's National Socialist Party and moved closer to the right wing pan-Arabist and anti-Hashemite Al Istiqlal (Independence) group whose members were supporters of Rashid Ali. Such was the origin of the Iraqi Baath, a right-wing Baath.

The peasant masses stayed out of this political arena until 1958. Not that the parties of the left had forgotten them. The communists made much of the need for agrarian reform — and so did the left-wing populists. And even Hikmat Sulaiman's Government had to make timid suggestions in this direction, until it was forced to retract and fell under the blows of the latifundist bourgeoisie. But the populist and communist actions could not reach the rural masses, because the latter were still profoundly divided by religious and national problems, and thus still dominated by their local ruling classes. The Kurdish North held a fifth of Iraq's population, organised into peasant clans. The national oppression of the Kurds helped to preserve the hold of this people's traditional chiefs and led to three major revolts against the Iraqi state: in 1927, under Sheikh Ahmed Barzani; in 1945, which saw an ephemeral Kurdish Republic of Iran; and in 1959, under Molla Moustapha Barzani. The communist and populist left could respect the legitimate aspirations of the Kurdish people — but the populist right of the Istiqlal and the Baath had always taken a pan-Arabist anti-Kurd position, thus playing into the hands of imperialism and the latifundist bourgeoisie. The south and the centre of the country were shared by three Arab groups of roughly equal importance: the Sunnite peasants of the centre, the Shiite peasants of the south and the desert nomads (Sunnite and Shiite). The latifundist bourgeoisie which had grown out of the traditional nomad chiefdoms — that is to say the (Sunnite and Shiite) sheikhs who had benefited from the agricultural improvements in the territory — were long able to use these divisions within the people to perpetuate their domination.

Thus the National Front which emerged in 1956-57 and which gave rise to the coup d'etat of 1958 remained an urban front which included the Istiqlal, the Baath, the National Democratic Party and the Communist Party. The intelligentsia and the urban masses organised by this front were resolutely anti-imperialist. They felt how urgent it was to drag Iraq out of its isolated provincialism, in view of the fact that struggles against French imperialism in Syria, against Zionism in Palestine and against the British occupation of the Suez Canal in Egypt (particularly during 1951, with the rejection of the treaty of 1936) were all linked with the Iraqi struggle against Britain, against the oil interests and their local clients, the Hashemite monarchy and the latifundist bourgeoisie. The revolt of the Palestinian people in 1936, the Zionist settlement and the creation of Israel in 1948, the imperialist-Zionist aggression against Egypt in 1956 were on each occasion the spark for popular revolts in Iraq, and on each occasion advanced the consciousness that the liberation of the East demanded the common struggle of all its people.

French imperialism in Syria was much less successful than that of the British in Iraq. Syria had no oil and there was no possibility of enhancing the value of agricultural land — which could have rallied the local bourgeoisie to the Mandate regime. This bourgeoisie was furthermore much more alive, at the end of the Ottoman era, than its equivalent in Iraq: so much so that it gave a 'levantine' tone to the whole area, based on an opening out onto the Mediterranean and therefore to the West. Under these conditions, French imperialism could only offer the Syrian bourgeoisie a mediocre development based on accentuated exploitation of the peasantry in the West of the country, trying to play on the existing religious divisions. But Syria suffered far more from the Zionist settlement in Palestine, for Syria and Palestine have always made up a single region of the Arab East. The bourgeois families of the area had always moved freely between Jerusalem, Damascus, Haifa and Beirut. The way the country had been split up between France and England in 1919, its Southern part having been turned over to Zionism by the Balfour Declaration in 1917, was completely artificial. The Syrian people resented this alienation almost as bitterly as the Palestinians themselves. The establishing of French power in Syria and Lebanon was difficult: the Druse revolt prolonged military insecurity right up to 1926. The National Arab Movement, organised since 1921 in a Syria-Palestine Committee formed in Geneva, transformed itself into a party which became a national force bringing together all the great families of the Syrian towns of Damascus, Aleppo, Homs and Hama: Shukri al Quvatly, Nazim Quds, Faiz el Khuri. The party won the 1928 elections and, as it stayed pro-independence, the French could find no suitable compromise, as the English had done in Iraq. The Assembly was dissolved in 1930 and the 1932 elections, despite the trickery involved, did not produce any political figures suitable for the sort of dialogue the French had in mind. The ascendency of the French Popular Front in 1936 seemed to offer some hope of viable negotiations, but projects for Franco-Syrian and Franco-Lebanese treaties were rejected by the French after two years of talks. The Syrians would not budge on the subject of Syrian-Lebanese unity — and since France could find more important allies in Lebanon than in Syria, it was determined to bargain separately with the two states. In fact the diversity of historical Syria goes back to ancient times. The region is shared by isolated agrarian communities, irredendist on the religious level but all

Arab culturally and linguistically: the Maronite Christians of Lebanon, the Lebanese Sunnites and Shiites, the Syrian Alids, the Sunnite peasantry of the Syrian West (Homs, Hana) on the one hand, the nomads and semi-nomads on the other.

In Lebanon the two parties of the levantine bourgeoisie, Emile Edde's Unionist Party and Bishara el Khuri's Constitutionalist Party, supported the idea of an independent Lebanon, a French client state. The only pro-Syrian pan-Arabist Unionist group, Antoun Saada's National Syrian Party refused to break with the bourgeoisie and remained very weak. Just before the War, it sought solace in a pro-fascist attitude and organised itself into phalanges. From these, certain more conscious tendencies evolved, much later, which participated in the setting up of the Syrian Baath.

Despite the failures of French policy in Syria, the country slid little by little into provincialism, thanks to the inadequate advantages granted by France to the Syrian bourgeoisie, which gradually also became a latifundist bourgeoisie. Nevertheless, the awakening of the urban Syrian population, its openings on to the outside world, made it possible to set up a pre-cocious Communist Party. Right from 1930, the leadership which still presides over the destiny of communism in the area was in control. Khaled Bagdache in Syria, Nicolas Shawi, Mustapha al Aris, Farajalla al Helw (assassinated in 1960), Antun Thabit in Lebanon. But the party never went beyond the rightist positions of support for the nationalist bourgeoisie, as is borne out by a programme which speaks only of independence and social justice, without daring to propose an agrarian reform, for fear of alienating the bourgeoisie.

France's collapse in 1940 created the right conditions for the elimination of imperialism in the area. The British occupiers looked on favourably during the anti-French demonstrations in 1943 and 1945, given that, as things were, no threat was being posed to the new imperialism. The attitude of the Gaullist Government, the bombing of Damascus and the Anglo-Russian intervention which followed led to Syrian and Lebanese independence in 1945. On the formal level this independence was more far-reaching than that of Iraq or Egypt, since the two new states were not tied to a foreign power by unequal treaties. British imperialism, having taken over, was able to draw support from the Syrian bourgeoisie much more openly than the French had been. But a new imperialism was soon to apply for the dominant role in the area: the imperialism of the United States. This is the real explanation for the series of coup d'etats in 1949: Husni al Zaim's in March, then Hinnawi's in August, finally Adib al Shishakli's in December, which ensured American supremacy and the withdrawal into Syrian provincialism of its servant, the dictatorship, until 1954.

The opportunism of Syrian communism not only furthered this process, it also left to others the choice of when to put an end to it. Whilst the Iraqi communists, in 1945, were busily organising the Jewish community of their country along anti-Zionist lines, the Syrian communists, and the majority of the Egyptian party, had by 1947 come round to the Soviet viewpoint which accepted the creation of Israel. This cost them six hard years of illegality, and their loss of prestige made it all the easier for the Baath to come to the fore. The origins of the latter go back to the Fifties, when the petty bourgeoisie of the provinces, especially of Hama, Homs and Lattaquie, gathered around the Republican Socialist Party formed by Akram el Hurani and Michel Aflaq. Their party campaigned for the agrarian reform which the communists had not dared to envisage. They thus undermined the Shishakli dictatorship and paved the way for the rise to power of the Baath from 1955 onwards. It was only then that Syria began to break out of its provincialist isolation.

From 1920 to 1948 imperialism reigned supreme in the whole area. In Egypt, in Syria and in Iraq, the agrarian and latifundist sections of the bourgeoisie, reinforced and made wealthy in the wake of imperialism, accepted the provincialist withdrawal to suit their foreign masters. This class was secure in its domination, since what opposition there was remained weak, without any real class basis of its own, a merely 'intelligentist' opposition, torn between its dissatisfaction — especially with the state of the country — and its attraction towards the pro-imperialist national bourgeoisie. The communists showed themselves incapable of understanding that the national bourgeoisie had completely sold out. They more or less willingly became little more than the left wing of this intelligentsia, thereby renouncing any real attempt to reach the proletarianised urban and rural masses. This was true both of the Egyptian communist movements (M.D.L.N., Fagr el Guedid, etc.) and of the 'powerful' Lebano-Syrian party. In fact the only exception was the Iraqi party under Fahd.

The treachery of the Arab latifundist bourgeoisie had as its corollary the abandonment of the Palestinian people, who were left to the tender mercies of the Zionist colonisation. It was the creation of the State of Israel in 1948, however, which sparked off the crisis of the imperialist system in the whole area, and renewed the class struggle.

THE PALESTINIAN QUESTION, 1920-1948

In Palestine, even during the Ottoman period, the Arab national movement could not but be anti-Zionist, could not fail to see the setting up of Kibbutzim in Palestine as the beginning of a European colonisation. The Ottoman administration, which was itself already semi-colonised, could offer little effective protection. Naively, the Arabs turned to the English during the War. In fact, the alliance between British imperialism and Zionism was already signed and sealed by the Balfour Declaration: Great Britain had decided to establish a European buffer-state in Palestine, in order to exert pressure on Egypt and to guarantee British control over

Suez. The Arab desert kinglets accepted the deal. Faycal, the eventual King of Iraq, was the first to commit open treachery, as the asking-price of his throne: in 1919 he signed an agreement with Weizman, which stipulated that 'in the drawing up of the constitution and in its administration, every step will be taken to ensure the implementation of the Balfour Declaration as indicated in these Faycal-MacMahon agreements.' The Zionists were not then asking for more than that.

During the whole period of the Mandate, the British authorities favoured the Zionist settlement. The people of Palestine protested; as early as 1920 there were demonstrations, assassinations, and savagely repressed riots. Shaken, the Arab ruling classes sold their lands to the Zionists. But the Arab peasants refused to do so, despite the great variety of pressures that were brought to bear on them. In 1947 the Zionists owned only 5.7% of the land. It was clear that only political power would enable them to evict the Arabs from their own country. During this period relations between Zionists and Arabs in Palestine gradually became those between coloniser and colonised. In 1935 the Arab population rebelled. The revolt lasted three years, beginning with a six months general strike and leading to a wide range of guerilla activities and the effective liberation of a large part of the territory. The colonialist-Zionists would probably not have been able to resist this upsurge by themselves: in fact the revolutionary movement was broken only by the British Army. It is quite clear that the Israeli victory of 1948 would not have been possible without this Arab defeat in 1936-1939. The revolt had been largely a popular and spontaneous one. The Arab ruling classes, in a panic, hastily organised a Palestinian High Council, chaired by Hadj Amin el Husseini, the treacherous Mufti of Jerusalem; with the complicity of the pro-imperialist Governments of Iraq, Egypt, etc., they helped imperialism disarm the revolution, by persuading the people of Britain's good intentions. Even then, however, the revolt of the Palestinian people had filled the masses in Iraq, Egypt and especially Syria, with a fervent enthusiasm; popular armed struggle had been shown to be the road to national liberation. How fraught with consequences was the failure of the Arab communists — still a mere handful it is true — to seize this historic occasion to lead the movement, to give it the organisational and ideological framework it needed.

Once the revolt had been broken, British imperialism, on the defensive and needing Arab neutrality during the War, played for time. Zionism understood that it needed a new protector — and found it in the United States. In 1947, under direct pressure from the United States, the United Nations proposed an exorbitant partition of Palestine, by which the Zionists, who had till then only been able to acquire 5.7% of the land, obtained 57% of the territory! American imperialism thus handed to Zionism the basis for its State.

Why did the Soviet Union support this partition plan, which was to compromise for twenty years the chances of communism in an area which the objective conditions were so favourable to it? This choice can only be explained in terms of a desire not to displease the Americans in a matter which then seemed of minor importance to Russian interests: in terms of Stalin's fundamental under-estimation of the potentialities of the Arab national liberation movement.

The Arab States themselves openly betrayed the Palestinian cause in 1947-1948. Emir Abdallah of Transjordan was soon negotiating the annexation of the West Bank to his desert kingdom which survived only thanks to British subsidies; King Farouk, faced with mounting pressure from the nationalist movement in his own country, hoped only for a classic diversion of politics into foreign affairs.

Abandoned and betrayed on all sides, the Palestinian people neverthless tried to resist: eventually they were beaten, despite the heroism of their resistance. The rest of the story is well known: consolidation of the racist and colonialist State of Israel, hundreds of thousands of Palestinians expelled from their country, land expropriation, etc.

3

THE ERA OF NASSERISM (1952-1967)

The next twenty years, from 1947 to 1967, were to be marked by three fundamental characteristics: firstly, the bankruptcy of the Arab national bourgeoisie and, thanks to the communists' opportunism, the rise of the nationalist petty bourgeoisie; secondly, the end of Britain's influence in the area, the growing role of the two superpowers, the US and the USSR, and the elaboration of a *modus vivendi* by which these two great powers could share out the area between themselves; thirdly, the affirmation of Zionist colonialism's expansionist character. The interaction between these three features was to determine the history of the period.

The mediocre withdrawal into provincialism of 1920-1947 rested on a social equilibrium based on a class alliance between the dominant imperialism of the area (Britain, and to a lesser extent France) and the latifundist bourgeoisie of the various states. This system could function as long as colonial enchantment of values ensured that some crumbs were left for the petty bourgeoisie. But internal contradictions set strict limits on this. These contradictions were apparent in the accelerated growth of the proletarianised and semi-proletarianised masses, from the First World War onwards; they were apparent in the ever increasing misery and unemployment, in the growth of a dissatisfied petty bourgeoisie, and, on the political level, in the emergence of new forces, especially the communist movement and the Muslim Brotherhood. In Syria and Iraq the same phenomenon expressed the existence of the same fundamental contradictions, but because the colonial inspired increase in (land) values was more recent in these countries, the final collapse came later there than in Egypt.

EGYPT

It was Egypt which inaugurated the new era, with the military coup d'etat of 1952. The changeover, from the old social relations based on the alliance between British imperialism and the latifundist and comprador bourgeoisies, to the new alliance between the Soviet State and Egyptian State Capitalism, was initiated by the agrarian reform of 1952. This programme of reform liquidated the power of the latifundists, gave the kulaks the leading role in the countryside and was extended in the nationalisations of 1957 and 1961, which first seized firms owned by Western capital, then those of Western capital's allies, the Egyptian bourgeoisie. The corollary of this programme was the gradual affirmation of a new ideology: Nasserism. Timidly at first, the emerging new Egyptian ruling class gradually broke away from the old bourgeoisie's policies of withdrawal into provincialism. The imperialist-Zionist aggression in 1956 forced this new class to react even more firmly and to affirm a clear pan-Arabism. The new regime tried for a long time to reach some internal compromise with the national bourgeoisie, and even sought to maintain the alliance with foreign imperialism. With American help, exploiting the weakness of British imperialism, the regime obtained in 1954 that which the Wafd had asked for in vain in 1950-1951: the evacuation of the British troops. But within a year the dominant American imperialism was pressuring the new Egyptian regime to join the anti-Soviet Baghdad Pact. Russian diplomacy was quick to exploit the spectacular proclamations on which the regime had previously committed itself on this subject. The Bandung Declaration and the delivery of Czech arms, in 1955, put a dent in the American system. The outcome was the World Bank's refusal to finance the Aswan Dam; Nasser's reply, the nationalisation of the Suez Canal in July; the tripartite Anglo-Franco-Israeli aggression launched in October; the American and Russian interposition; and the regime's drift into state capitalism in 1957.

What was the attitude of Egyptian communists during this evolution? At the time of the coup d'etat, most of the communist organisations had taken up positions opposed to the new regime; hardly surprising, since the first act of the latter had been to hang Moustapha Khamis and his companions, the leaders of the striking workers of Kafr-el-Dawar. Nasserism's undemocratic style, particularly noticeable in 1958 with the eviction of General Naguib, had led the majority of Egyptian communists to label it fascist and demagogic and to accuse it of treachery in the Sudan and in the negotiation of the treaty agreement on Suez. Then came a short period of reconciliation, motivated by the nationalisation of the Suez Canal and the other early nationalisations.

Later still, from 1959 to 1964, the communists were again to pay dearly and to suffer massive arrests, for their opposition to what had become regime policy in Syria as in Egypt, namely bureaucratic repression and a total clamp-down on all attempts at autonomous popular expression. Nevertheless, from 1964 onwards, Egyptian communism kept its criticisms to itself and finally came round to a collaborationist policy.

It would be unfair to accuse Egyptian communism as a whole of opportunism. Some of the very first analyses of that phenomenon which was later to become so important in the Third World, namely the formation of a dependent state bourgeoisie, were formulated in Egypt right back in the late Fifties, although by minority voices, it is true. But Egyptian communism was ideologically disarmed by revisionist theses, the true nature of which it failed to grasp. These theses reinforced the opportunist tendencies within the communist movement, and, in combination with the mainly petty bourgeois character of that movement, were the main causes of its decomposition from 1965 onwards.

As for the ideological evolution of Nasserism, it reflects, in its contradictions and in its poverty, the double failure of the liberal bourgeoisie and of the proletarian masses: the failure represented by the bourgeoisie's betrayal and by the proletariat's inability to affirm an ideological hegemony. On the ideological level, Nasserism, far from pursuing and furthering the radical tendencies of bourgeois nationalism, such as those of the left wing of the Wafd for example, chose rather to link itself with the reactionary tendencies of the petty bourgeoisie, notably with the Muslim Brotherhood, whose anti-democratic style Nasserism shared. The measures which Nasserism introduced on the level of social and economic organisation, such as the agrarian reforms and the nationalisations, were soon to become inconsistent with its ideological formulations.

In the final analysis, it is Egyptian communism which must bear the responsibility for this confused state of affairs. The objective conditions of the period made it quite possible for the proletariat and poor peasantry not only to take the political lead in the movement but also to affirm their ideological hegemony. The petty bourgeois character of the original communist movement could have been changed quite easily; had the movement really become the party of the proletariat, it would have managed to exercise that hegemony and to free itself from revisionist confusion, as happened in Vietnam. By remaining petty bourgeois, on the contrary, the communist movement was itself to reinforce revisionism and thus find itself in the same boat as Nasserism. Under these conditions neither Nasserism nor the communist movement could understand the nature of their own policy, its perspectives, or the reasons for the failure to which it was leading. As these two movements came closer together, from 1964 onwards, they became more and more the prisoners and the victims of the same nationalist petty bourgeois way of seeing their own actions; actions which they believed either actually were or would lead to the transition to socialism. The few lucid minds who struggled against this confusion remained very isolated.

The same characteristics reappear, for the same basic reasons, when we turn to examine the other Arab countries, especially Syria and Iraq.

SYRIA

The Egyptian example had a considerable impact in the Arab East. In Syria, following the fall of the Shishakli dictatorship in 1954, a heterogeneous coalition came to power: the new petty bourgeois social forces of the Baath, supported by the Communist Party, on the one hand, the forces of the traditional bourgeoisie of the national bloc on the other. In September 1954 Khaled Bakdache, the first communist member of an Arab Parliament, was elected, and several others became MPs with communist support. Soon after the 1956 war the new Syrian regime, finding itself incapable of coping with the upsurge of popular forces, (which in Syria were particularly sensitive to the Palestinian cause) handed the country over to Nasser. The U.A.R., inaugurated in February 1958, the product of Syrian and Egyptian unity, had as its first consequence the elimination of the Syrian communists. It only lasted three years: already in 1961 the Syrian bourgeoisie had begun to exploit the errors and unpopularity of the Egyptian bureaucracy. The agrarian reforms carried out in 1958 on the Egyptian model were called into question, as were the nationalisations. But the victory of the traditional Syrian bourgeoisie was to be shortlived, for the rising forces of the petty bourgeoisie had already created an irreversible situation. The 1963 coup d'etat brought the Syrian Baath back into power, and this time it stood alone. The development of the new state capitalism got under way again. From the first 1960-65 plan, which was still based on the illusion of an active participation of Syrian and Western private capital, to the 1965-70 plan, which gave a predominant role to nationalisations and Russian aid, one sees the same evolution as that which took place in Egypt between the pre-1957 period and the 1960-65 plan period. In 1966 a new coup d'etat set the seal on this drift, by bringing to power the left wing of the Baath as symbolised by Salah Jdid. Syria's satellitisation by the USSR was confirmed in Western eyes, particularly when the Syrian Government persistently interfered with the Iraq Petroleum Company pipeline.

The inadequacies of Syrian communism are behind the success of the Baath. In this respect it is significant that the founder of the Baath, Michel Aflaq, who was a communist sympathiser in the Thirties, broke with the Syrian Communist Party following his disappointment with the French *Front Populaire* and with the Party leadership's blatant opportunism at the time. Rejecting Marxism and giving absolute priority to Arab unity, the Baath (created in 1943 by Aflaq and Salah Bitar) was to stay politically equivocal until its fusion with Akram el Hurani's Socialist Party in 1953 — a party which was actually more nationalist than socialist. The scene was then set for an *entente* with Nasserism. After the failure of the union between Egypt and Syria, the Syrian Baath broke into pro-Nasser and anti-Nasser factions; in fact these factions were enemy twin brothers, sharing the same ideology, the same vision, the same perspective. This vision necessarily brought them closer to the revisionist communists, with whom they differed on no essential point, despite some minor quarrels concerning the distribution of power.

For basically the same reasons the Baath movement was eventually able to spread beyond Syria, notably to Iraq. The thirty years of nationalism leading up to the 1958 coup and the fact that Iraq had no liberal bourgeois tradition, nor any equivalents of the left wings of the Wafd and the Syrian nationalist parties, made it easy for the Baath to grow in Iraq; it was the only force of its kind. The Iraqi Baath was clearly the legitimate heir to petty bourgeois populism. But, in the last analysis, the retreat of the Iraqi Communist Party after the assassination of Fahd had the same decisive effect as the equivalent failures in Egypt and Syria: the communists, by sinking into revisionism, gave the Baath the opportunity to seize the leadership of the movement.

Even in faraway Morocco the opportunism of the communists led to the same results. The success of the left wing of the U.N.F.P. was only possible because of the timidity of the Communist Party. This is the only possible explanation for the penetration of the Baath in that country, as in Tunisia, for the same reasons. The 'terrorist' option chosen by Mohamed Basri from 1965 onwards, with Ghadaffi's help, and the repeated attempts to assassinate the King, which have been substituted for mass action, are quite simply the unmistakable mark of a failure, the failure of Nasserist petty bourgeois nationalism.

IRAQ

The same was true in Iraq. The front constituted in 1957 overthrew the Hashemite-latifundist bourgeois authorities in the July 1958 coup d'etat. From 1958 to 1963 the new regime wavered between a Nasserist-type right-wing line and a left-wing line. One must remember that in Iraq events had not unfolded in quite the same way as in Egypt or Syria. On the one hand the Anglo-Hashemite domination had been absolute and long lasting; on the other hand the Communist Party had been less opportunist than elsewhere. Also, the popular masses were quick to intervene. The 'forces of popular resistance' — militias — settled old scores and liquidated the latifundist bourgeoisie. Kassem, the leader of the new state, soon put an end to these actions, but was then almost overthrown from the right: Abdel Salam Aref was eliminated in the nick of time, in September 1958; Shawwaf attempted a putsch in March 1959. That putsch having failed, the regime purged itself of the right-wing Baath and Istiqlal elements which had gathered around Rachid Ali el Gaylani, Fouad Rikabi, Abdel Salam Aref and Shawwaf. The supporters of Abdel Karim Kassem, the old guard of the National Democratic Party, were thus left to face the Communist Party by themselves — and here too a programme of agrarian reform eliminated the old latifundist bourgeoisie, to some extent at any rate. It even seemed possible that the regime's attempt at a *rapprochement* with the Kurds, the amnesty and return from the USSR of Mustapha Barzani, and the creation of the Democratic Party of the Iraqi Kurds could inaugurate a new era and bring about the definitive democratic solution of the Kurdish national problem.

But Kassem was constantly manoeuvring, seeking to protect the right-wing forces. For a long time he refused to have communist Ministers in the Government and tried to play on the split in the Communist Party brought about by Daud Sayegh's opportunist fraction. No one really knows what happened at Kirkouk in July 1959. Was it a massacre of innocent Turkomans or of right-wing henchmen? Was it a deliberate provocation used by the right-wing Baath? Or was it the mistaken action of irresponsible popular elements (the belated explanation of the Communist Party)? What we do know is that Kassem used it as an excuse to eliminate the Communist Party from the Government and to break the 1961 strikes, thus alienating himself from the working masses. Furthermore, in the summer of 1961, the Kurdist revolt re-ignited, the Baghdad regime having failed for too long to meet the demands for autonomy. Kassem attempted to create for himself a new popularity by raising the problem of Kuwait, a territory which had been part of the Iraqi Vilayet of Basra under the Ottomans, had then been conceded to the British as a protectorate in 1913 and had become, since the Second World War, one of the world's richest oil states. But Kassem's efforts were all in vain; isolated, he was brought down by Abdel Salam Aref's 1963 coup d'etat and assassinated by his old partner of 1958.

The regime which followed was right-wing and petty bourgeois, in the mediocre tradition of Rashid Ali al Gaylani. Inaugurated by a blood bath — the massacre of thousands of communist militants, workers, peasants and left-wing intellectuals — the regime, by November 1963, had already got rid of those of its Baathist elements it judged to be still too far to the left. It put an end to both the agrarian reform programme and the policy of state capitalist development, compensating for its capitulation to imperialism and its internal allies by an Arab demagogy, e.g. the dispute over Chatt-El-Arab, claimed by both Iran and Iraq, regular hangings of 'agents of Zionism', etc. At the same time it became embroiled in the repression of Kurdistan. Nasser's Government was always a ready ally for the new regime: had Shawwaf's 1959 coup in Mossoul succeeded, the Egyptian Army, stationed in Syria, would have been called in to set the seal on the fusion of Iraq and the U.A.R.

PALESTINE AND ISRAEL

In 1948 as in 1956 it was Israeli expansionism which unmasked the real nature of the latifundist and comprador bourgeoisie of the Arab states; this bourgeoisie was revealed as a collaborator with imperialism, and its pan-Arabism was shown to be demagogic, intermittent and purely verbal. Israeli expansionism, a threat to the frontiers of its neighbours, also forced each state out of isolationism. In 1948 as in 1956 the Israeli aggressions provoked the Arab masses to revolt against their governments. But, because the communists had not understood the deeply pro-imperialist nature of their countries' national bourgeoisies, because they chose an opportunist line and would not call for a popular armed struggle under the ideological leadership of the proletariat as the only way of overthrowing imperialist oppression, they facilitated the transfer of power from this latifundist comprador bourgeoisie to the petty bourgeoisie. In this they were helped by the state policy of the Soviet Union. The USSR, having become a world power, saw the Arab East only as an area situated on its southern flank and dominated by its American adversary. It chose to break this bastion, and in order to do so based its action on those political groups and social strata which seemed the most useful in the short term. The theoretical explanation for this policy — 'national democracy' and the 'non-capitalist road' — is based, here as elsewhere, on one simple ambition: to draw specific Third World countries out of the American sphere of influence without endangering the policy of peaceful co-existence by the extension of socialist revolution. Consciously or not, the communist parties of the Arab world, by adopting the Moscow line, betrayed and disarmed their masses and pointed the way to state capitalism.

Russian diplomacy enjoyed some considerable successes during the period: Egypt, Syria, and to some extent Iraq, were detached from the Western system. Little by little a new *status quo* was established in the East. The Russians got the two or three states mentioned, the Americans got the oil-producing states of the Arabian peninsula. The equilibrium was maintained by the Arab-Israeli *modus vivendi:* Israel, supported by Western imperialism, was to refrain from aggression; in exchange, the Arab states were to prevent the Palestinian people from challenging Zionist colonisation.

From 1947 to 1967 the Arab states actively sought to keep their side of the bargain: to prevent the Palestinian people from carrying on a struggle which could only be revolutionary. The Jordanian and Egyptian administrations in Arab Palestine fulfilled this function. From 1948 to 1955 silence was imposed on the Palestinian victims of the defeat. But Ben Gurion, on returning to power in 1955, declared that he only accepted to form a Cabinet on condition that all possible efforts be made for an expansion to the South. Threatened directly, Egypt was forced to react. It attempted to do so in the manner which would least upset the *modus vivendi:* by organising commando groups, the *fedayin*, under Egyptian command, in order to put pressure on Israel to renounce expansionism. But Egypt clearly did not want this means of pressure to escape its control; the Palestinians were not allowed to organise themselves for their liberation: they were kept a herd of refugees. Seeking to draw profit from a combination of circumstances in 1956, Israel attempted to annex Sinai with Anglo-French support. French involvement in the attempt was rooted in the Algerian War, whilst the British hoped to return to a Middle East from whence they had been driven out by the United States. The agreements between Russia and the US eventually forced the British, French and

Israeli trrops to withdraw, and the Arab states resumed their policy of keeping to commitments and repressing the Palestinian people. But the same internal dynamic which had pushed Israeli colonialism into expansionism reasserted its influence. The growing crisis in Jewish immigration led Israel, from 1963 onwards, into new preparations for attacks against its Arab neighbours: by diverting the waters of the Jordan and by threats of preventive war, Israel paved the way for 1967. The Arab states' reply was the creation,in 1964, of the Palestine Liberation Organisation. That in fact this P.L.O. was feeble and incapable of mobilising the people of Palestine to participate in their own liberation, that its function was on the contrary to prevent them doing so, is amply confirmed by the fact that the Arab states, at the Alexandria summit meeting, conferred the leadership of the Organisation on Ahmad el Shukeiri, a garrulous demagogue. The so-called Palestine Liberation Army remained an integral part of the Arab armies. The P.L.O. brought together in its bureaucratic structures those bourgeois and petty bourgeois elements which had long been by-passed by history and which had already betrayed the liberation struggle of their people during the 1936-39 revolt.

At the same time, the internal contradictions particular to the development of state capitalism in Egypt, Syria and Iraq made for a radicalisation of the regimes in those countries, where mass pressure was making itself felt from 1964 onwards. The Israeli intervention, aimed at putting an end to this leftward drift, highlighted the role of policeman which imperialism had assigned to Israel in the area.

There are profound reasons for the double failure of this Arab petty bourgeoisie, for its failure against Israel and its failure on the level of Arab unity. In analysing the ideology of the 'new class', its forms of government and the stages by which it constituted itself in Egypt, Mahmoud Hussein makes the following point: state capitalism, because it is a capitalism, must remain within the capitalist world system. It thus cannot really break with imperialism. Belonging to the world system then perpetuates underdevelopment, ruins any changes for independence or real development. To substitute the Soviet Union for the United States as the commercial partner and source of capital (so-called 'aid') in no way changes this fundamental relation of dependency. The petty bourgeoisie, which brings local dependent state capitalism to the fore, thus becomes the main link in the transmission of imperialist domination, thereby replacing the old latifundist-comprador bourgeoisie which introduced dependent private capitalism in the previous period. The ideological vacuity of the petty bourgeoisie, and its profound acculturation, are clear indications of its function: to introduce bourgeois ideology on a world scale.

The socialism of this new dependent class is only a mask and is quite incapable of mobilising the masses: this is the real explanation for the weakness of the Arab armies. In the same way, the call to Arab unity proposed by these classes is totally insincere. That unity can only be a unity of struggle against imperialism. The masses can hardly liberate themselves from imperialism within the narrow framework of states which are the product of that imperialism. This is why the petty bourgeoisie, having become a state bourgeoisie, has never really sought to promote Arab unity. The most advanced of these bourgeoisies has at the most attempted to conquer the others; hence the abuses of the Egyptian bourgoisie in Syria, its pretensions in Iraq and the reaction of the peoples and bourgeoisies of those countries, which in the end played into the hands of imperialism.

THE 1967 WAR AND THE END OF NASSERISM

The acceleration of the internal contradictions of Israeli society between 1956 and 1967, the decrease in Jewish immigration, the social and racial conflicts between Oriental and Western Jews, and the dangerous possibility of a radicalisation of the Nasserist regime all led to the Israeli aggression of June 1967. The Israeli military victory, the annexation of Jordanian, Syrian and Egyptian territories, bringing the number of Arabs subjected to Israeli colonialism up from 300,000 in June 1967 to 1,300,000, finally disrupted the *status quo* on which the repartition of the area between the US and the USSR was based. These superpowers immediately had the UN pass the resolution of the 22nd November 1967, which called for the withdrawal of Israeli troops from all territories occupied during the aggression. This resolution, which was accepted by the main Arab states, notably Egypt and Jordan, resolved nothing, since it left the aggressive colonialist potential of Zionism intact. But the Israel of 1967 was not the Israel of 1956. Israeli micro-imperialism had grown stronger and no longer felt obliged to renounce its victory. The Arab states were thus immediately brought face to face with their own people, and their margin for manoeuvre was shown to be very narrow. For all the daily promises of a reconquest of Sinai by the regular armies, each passing day brought home the impossibility of this project. Each day brought home the fact that military superiority remained in the hands of the Israeli army, whose air force could, with impunity, fly over Upper Egypt, bomb Cairo, violate Syrian air space and destroy the Beirut airport.

The Liberation Movement in Palestine

Furthermore, the Israeli victory freed the Palestinian people from the yoke of the Arab bureaucracies and finally gave it itself the possibility of launching a revolutionary struggle for its liberation. As the first victim of Zionist colonial oppression, the Palestinian people had in fact never had any other choice. Right from before the Second World War the Palestinians had been far more radicalised than the other Arab peoples.

The Communist Party of Palestine, founded in the Twenties by a few Jewish intellectuals, had become progressively Arabised during the Thirties; at the time, the Communist International still played a revolutionary role, as is borne out by the calls for the Arabisation of the Party from 1924 onwards. Faced with the treachery of the Arab ruling classes, the Communist Party had become the only Arab party of national liberation; however it had not gained sufficient strength by 1936-39 to turn the revolt into an invincible revolution under its leadership. The World War, the Russian policy of appeasement towards Western imperialism, and after the War, Russian State policy had then led Palestinian communism into degeneration. During the War, the Party had turned into a vague 'national front' and with the recognition of the 1947 partition an Israeli party had appeared, a party whose fate it was (or that of its Jewish fraction at least), to accept an eventual collapse into Zionism. The Arab masses had then been thrown into disarray. As helpless emigrants, the Palestinians at first attempted to participate in the political life of the neighbouring countries to which they had fled, especially in Jordan, Syria and Lebanon, where they were to be the basis for the leftward drift of the Baath. Later they sought to organise themselves as Palestinians. The brief experience of 1956, when, during a few months, they were left alone against Israel, without Arab protection, was to be a fruitful lesson during which they relearnt to do battle. It was from this experience that El Fatah, the great organisation of the Palestinian people's struggle, was born on the 1st January 1959. In 1965 El Fatah and its military wing, El Assifa, launched an armed struggle. The June War swept aside the puppets in the P.L.O.; El Fatah became the leadership of the Palestinian people's liberation struggle. The battle of Karame, in March 1968, made the Palestinian people into the main obstacle to Israeli colonialism. El Fatah's goal, an independent and democratic Palestinian State in which all citizens — Jews and Arabs — would be equal, not only in law but also in fact, presupposed an elimination of racial and colonial privilege, and hence an elimination of the capitalist system on which that privilege was based. This goal defined the only possible revolutionary perspective.

Struggle, and struggle alone, will eventually decide the definitive form of a solution to the problems of the Middle East; it may be a unitary or binational state, it may be a Middle East confederation, or it may be something else. Whatever the outcome, to quarrel about these issues today is objectively to play into the hands of those who seek to delay the anti-imperialist struggle.

El Fatah is not the only organisation of the Palestinian struggle. The Popular Front for the Liberation of Palestine, which grew out of the Baath in Syria around 1960, has also stressed that the Palestinian people must be the main agent responsible for its own cause. Its left wing, the Popular Democratic Front for the Liberation of Palestine, stresses its Marxist-Leninist orientation but does not set itself apart from the Fatah when it comes to action. Indeed the various organisations of the struggle have formed a common Palestinian National Council.

The Palestinian people's increasing role in the struggle has radically changed the parameters of the problem, not only in Palestine but also in the adjacent Arab territories (mainly Jordan and Lebanon) where most of the Arab refugees are concentrated, and even in the Arab world as a whole. The puppet state of Transjordan, which had been handed over to Emir Abdallah who became King in 1946, had had no real political life till its annexation of the Palestinian West Bank in 1948. The traitor Abdallah (killed in 1951 for his collusion with Israel), his son Talal, then his grandson Hussein gradually lost control. The League of National Liberation, an offshoot of Palestinian communism, was at first — from 1949 to 1955 — the only really organised political force in the country. But its opportunist line — 'overthrow the regime in Amman before attacking Israeli colonialism' — prevented it reaching out to the masses and restricted it to intellectual circles. During the crisis of 1956 the way was clear for a Jordanian 'Nasserism', as symbolised by the short-lived Government under Sulaiman al Nabulsi, which enjoyed the support of the League communists. The eventual liquidation of this Government by King Hussein brought home the vanity of the hopes placed in such a policy. El Fatah was quick to draw the appropriate conclusions, and organised its own revolutionary power base in Jordan, both in the camps and outside, to carry on the armed struggle in occupied Palestine.

The Revival of Arab Nationalism

Even small and peaceful Lebanon was to have its political life disordered by the arrival on the scene of the Palestinian people. Till then, Lebanon had not undergone the transformations which had led the petty bourgeoisie to adopt state capitalism in Syria, Iraq and Egypt. Lebanon's specific role within the imperialist system of the area — its function as a refuge for capital and as a tourist playground—led people to believe that this 'Switzerland of the Middle East' would never be affected by the people's struggle for liberation. Neither the fall in 1952 of Bishara el Khuri, the representative of the corrupt plutocracy which ensured the smooth operation of the system, nor the challenge to Camille Chamoun in 1958, nor the disembarkation and then departure of the American marines during the summer of the same year, brought about any real change. But in 1967 everything altered, from the moment the Palestinian refugees in Lebanon took up a combative stance. Since then the Lebanese State has no longer been such a safe refuge for the capital of Arab emirs and 'socialist' bureaucrats. The Arabian peninsula, the Sudan, Libya and the faraway Maghreb were in their turn affected by the emerging role of the Palestinian people. By then, the time when the oil companies and nomad sheikhs ruled as absolute masters of the Arabian peninsula was already over. Saudi

Arabia, created following the expulsion of Sherif Hussein of Mecca, after the First World War, was still, it is true, the Kingdom of Aramco. But there were already urban nuclei, both proletarian and petty bourgeois, which had forced the ruling family to make some concessions. The fall of Yemen's Imam Badr in September 1962, the popular riots in South Yemen and the reinforcement of the national liberation movement of the area brought the ancient kingdom of Saba into the modern world. Neither the Saudis' constant intervention on the side of tribes faithful to Badr, nor the Egyptian intervention of 1962-67, which supported the moderate elements of the republican regime (Sallal, then Cadi Abdel Rahman el Iriani) succeeded in liquidating the new republic. On the contrary, the lessons of the relative defeat of the revolutionary forces in Yemen were drawn by the South-Yemenites who, in checking British attempts to perpetuate the country's division into micro-sultanates, were led to more radical positions.

Although somewhat marginal in the affairs of the Arab world, Sudan was also affected by the national liberation movement. The hand-over of local power to the traditional ruling classes — the semi-feudalists of the religious fraternities, Ansar and Ashiqqa — in keeping with the Anglo-Egyptian Agreements of 1953, failed to ensure a stable domination for imperialism. The popular movement grew; the communists, who had been organised since 1944, the working class — notably the powerful railway-men's union — and the qualified petty bourgeoisie were all quick to express their discontent; and with the fall of pseudo-parliamentarianism and later Abboud's military dictatorship, which had sought to base its power on the urban petty bourgeoisie, the urban and rural masses in turn entered the struggle. The endemic rebellion of the non-Arab South is the semi-spontaneous, semi-manipulated answer of the peasantry to oppression by imperialism and its tool, the Northern bureaucracy — and this rebellion is at the same time imperialism's lever against the said bureacracy. The Sudanese communists and democrats, of both North and South, have always taken the correct position on this issue: denouncing the oppression of the peoples of the South, without falling into the traps set by imperialism and its Southern agents. They have always counterposed the possibility of a popular unity based on mutual respect of particularities to the cul-de-sac of forced assimilation.

Even Libya, desert kingdom of the oil companies, was marked by the emerging role of the Palestinians. The coup d'etat which replaced the ageing monarchy with a team of petty bourgeois military officers was largely the result of the Israeli aggression of 1967.

For a long time the Maghreb had been set apart from the currents which had swept through the Arab East; this was due not only to French colonialism which created specific forms of oppression and local problems, but also to geographical distnace and local particularities — notably the 'Berberism' of the Maghreb. Probably because of the backwardness of the development of French capital, and because French domination of Algeria had begun long before imperialism, the country had been partially settled by a colony of 'poor whites'. The same system had been used in Morocco and Tunisia. It was only afterwards that the more advanced forms of colonisation developed in the Maghreb, particularly in Morocco; forms characterised by investments of French finance capital in mining and even in industry. The Algerian landed aristocracy had long been pushed out of the picture — more so, in fact, by the activities of Abd el Kader (1830-48) than by French colonisation. In Morocco, on the contrary, the landed aristocracy was reinforced by colonisation, while Tunisia shared characteristics of both the two cases above. Even if these structures are now becoming less and less important in the face of the rise of the petty bourgeoisie in all three countries, they have nonetheless had a long lasting effect on the national movement. The war of extermination conducted until 1848, during the conquest of Algeria, gave a pronounced popular peasant character to the Algerian resistance, and led to the destruction and mass emigration of the urban elites. The new urban strata re-created by colonisation had no links with either the countryside or the old urban ruling classes. This explains the superficiality of their nationalism and their assimilationist demands, as defined by Ferhat Abbas even after the Second World War. The opposition of the *Pieds Noirs* closed this option. Little by little the resistance movement shifted its base to the cities and the immigrant workers in France. From this movement there emerged the armed insurrection of 1954 — and it was during the Algerian War (1954-62) that Algerian nationalism was really reborn. This hiatus (1850-1945) between the old period of Algerian nationalism and its contemporary rebirth did not occur in Tunisia and Morocco, which were colonised later, and therefore the modern nationalist movement in these countries lacked the popular antecedents it had in Algeria.

In Tunisia, the national movement, which grew up during the Thirties amongst bourgeois and petty bourgeois strata, never entertained any assimilationist illusions. But it was always bourgeois and moderate, as symbolised by the man to whose name it has been linked right from its origins, Bourguiba. When this movement found itself overtaken by the revolt of the peasant masses in 1954, the situation was brought back under control thanks to the French policy of making concessions which led up to independence in 1956. In Morocco, which had been colonised even later an even more marked continuity was apparent. This explains why the modern urban nationalist movement was to line up behind the country's traditional elites, which provided its leadership right up to independence.

As the long night of French colonisation came to an end, the Maghreb, isolated from the Oriental Arab world, found it difficult to regain its own personality. Its nationalism was then still purely local, although some awareness of belonging to the wider Arab world had survived. The political evolution of the states of the Maghreb during the period 1960-70, highlighted the clash between the deep social realities and an apparent political reality shaped by the vicissitudes of colonisation. The Algerian national movement, having reached the heights of its radicalism during the first years of the war of independence, was eventually taken over by the petty bourgeoisie, which ultimately became the main beneficiary of independence. In Tunisia, under the growing influence of the rising petty bourgeoisie, the Destour slipped slowly from capitalist liberalism to 'National Socialism'. In Morocco, the regime has still not managed to stabilise itself: petty bourgeois pressure almost carried the day in 1960, and the failure of these pressures explains the return of more traditional conservative forces. Algeria and Tunisia have practically finished their process of evolution, from moderate nationalism in Tunisia and revolutionary peasant radicalism in Algeria, to national socialism. Morocco has not yet closed this chapter of its history, but the social and political forces of petty bourgeois socialism are already on the move there.

1967 brought out the bankruptcy of the petty bourgeois nationalist powers through which imperialism — and hence underdevelopment — had been perpetuated. The Soviet alliance was shown to be a temporary product of circumstance. Notwithstanding the considerable internal contradictions which this alliance brought to the fore within Arab society, the fact remains that the global strategy into which this alliance was integrated (so-called non-capitalist development) was inevitably doomed to fail.

The Israeli aggression of 1967 brought an end to the *status quo* of the twenty previous years. Ironically, this aggression, which Israel saw as a means of consolidating the *status quo* by forcing the Arab states to accept it once and for all, in fact had precisely the opposite effect. The Israeli victory served only to unmask the impotence of bourgeois and petty bourgeois nationalism, be it supported by the West or by the USSR, be it based on local liberal capitalism or on state capitalism. The aggression liberated one force only: that of the Palestinian people. In so doing, it inaugurated a new era in the Arab world, the era of the common struggle by the peoples of the area against imperialism and Zionism, a struggle which in the end can only merge with the fight for socialist revolution.

Nevertheless, one must lucidly re-examine the ideological nature of Arab nationalism's reaction to the successive defeats of 1948 and 1967, since it reveals the blind alley which a petty bourgeois direction leads into. The violent reaction following 1948 resulted in the constitution of the Arab Nationalist Movement (Harakat el Qawmiyin) by various strands of the intelligentsia (Palestinians, Lebanese, Syrians and others) gathered at Beirut. The slogan 'Arab unity first' was a natural outcome. Nor was there anything surprising in the movement's *rapprochement* with Nasserism and the Baath in 1958-61. Nasser's failure in Syria led to the growth of an autonomous left wing in 1964, and the 1967 defeat consolidated it. All the attempts to transcend Nasserism came out of this movement. But what happened to these attempts? The first organisation formed following 1967, the P.F.L.P., although violently anti-Nasserist, anti-Baathist and even anti-Fatah, never developed any real social perspective. It denounced the betrayal but failed to understand its class nature. To treat this attitude as simply the product of a personality such as George Habash, a graduate of the American University of Beirut with an anti-communist nationalist past, is in no way sufficient explanation. Will the P.D.F.L.P., created by Nayef Hawatmeh two years later, embark on a critique of nationalism from a new class position, in theory and in practice? It remains to be seen. In South Yemen, a movement which came out of the extreme left wing of the Qawmiyin carried things further than anywhere else. But, amongst the Palestinian people itself, the P.D.F.L.P. has so far progressed very little beyond the limits of a nationalist movement. In Lebanon, the Lebanese Communist Action Organisation, for all its Marxist-Leninist proclamations and the stress it places on the Chinese Cultural Revolution, is still only a small *coterie* of intellectuals. Furthermore, however attractive the Rejection Front may seem in the wake of 1973, it is hardly a substitute for a genuine and correct mass strategy. Indeed, it is the practical inadequacy of these actions, at best only the embryo of a revolutionary programme, which lies behind the renewal of Black September's desperate terrorism.

4

THE ARAB FUTURE: BOURGEOIS NATIONALISM OR REVOLUTION

FROM THE DEFEAT OF 1967 TO THE VICTORY OF 1973: A RESPITE FOR THE ARAB BOURGEOISIE

Until the defeat of June 1967 the Arab world presented a picture whose broad lines were after all quite simple, the key features being the irresistible rise of the national liberation movement. This movement had successively drawn Egypt, the Mashreq and the Maghreb into a series of victorious struggles, as symbolised by the restoration of independence and the liquidation of the old feudal and comprador regimes. It had an ideology and a model in Nasserist Egypt and it had Nasser himself as its charismatic leader. The popular masses had little consciousness of this petty bourgeois nationalist movement's inherent weaknesses. The 1948 defeat in Palestine could be palmed off as due to now defunct neo-colonial regimes. The gradual installation of dependent state capitalism was on the whole confused with the transition to socialism, and most of the communists accepted the confusion and little by little came round to supporting the 'progressive' new regimes; their occasional criticisms of the 'negative aspects' of the new order never really explored the real dynamic and the sort of future which was in the offing. The defeat of 1967 was like a bolt of lightning revealing these intrinsic weaknesses. Was the Nasserist system then no better than King Farouk's? The defeat unleashed a storm of criticism — not only from the Palestinians but also from the latent forces which till then had been kept under by the flood of Nasserist rhetoric. The defeat was a reminder of the importance of both the Palestinian question and Arab unity. Areas which had only just begun to participate in the era of independence — the Maghreb, the Sudan, the Arabian peninsula — found themselves immediately forced to take a position on the great conflicts of the Arab world. In Egypt and the Mashreq, the much older national liberation movement had settled the problems such as that of independence long before the vital questions concerning the future presented themselves: the questions of Arab unity, of its capacity to assert itself on the world chessboard (and thus to put an end to the Zionist challenge); the question of the class nature of the regime and of the corresponding development strategy. Elsewhere the transition from the old problems to the new was far more abrupt.

The defeat of 1967 could have opened up a new period, a period of socialist revolution. But there was no sufficiently coherent revolutionary force to carry out such a task, not in Egypt, not in the Mashreq, not even in Palestine. The ravages of Nasserism were to prove very costly. The absence of new radical forces allowed a respite to the Arab bourgeoisies. To redress the balance in their favour these bourgeoisies first had to liquidate any embryo of revolutionary development, especially in Palestine. Once this was accomplished, the scene was set for a return to diplomacy and then for military revenge, thus creating the conditions for a renewed alliance with imperialism. Once the credibility of the Arab bourgeoisies had been re-established by the victory of 1973 and by the efficacious use of the oil weapon, the Arab world entered a new phase of its history, characterised by the eclipse of Nasserism.

The Liquidation of the Threat of Palestinian Revolution

For the Arab bourgeoisies the immediate danger was the revolutionary situation created in Palestine by the June War. However two years sufficed for the Jordanian regime to liquidate, in the short term, the threat represented by the Palestinian movement. In Lebanon, in October 1969, the battles between the Palestinian refugees and Government forces came to an end following the agreement signed between the leader of the Fatah, Yasser Arafat, and the Lebanese commanders: the disarming of the Palestinians soon followed. In Jordan the great trial of strength began in January 1970. In June a mediation commission (Egypt, Algeria, Libya, Sudan) separated the antagonists. In September fighting broke out again and reached its climax with the battle of Amman, which the Palestinians lost. The Hussein-Arafat agreement, signed in Cairo on the 27th September on the eve of Nasser's death, confirmed the defeat. By January the Palestinian bases established in Jordan had been totally destroyed.

The revolutionary Arab left is still quarrelling over who was to blame for this defeat. The minority movements (P.F.L.P. and P.D.F.L.P.) accuse Arafat and the Fatah of having entertained petty bourgeois illusions which led to an unwarranted reliance on an Arab united front: on the contrary, they say, the treachery of the allies, Nasser or Hussein, was to be expected and no one should have been misled by illusions of pan-Arab patriotism. However if one examines what these minority movements propose and what they have actually done, one cannot help noticing the weakness of their analyses, which are based on a single perspective, that of socialist revolutionary armed struggle. The theory of the *foco* (focus) as formulated by Che Guevara reduces the perspective of revolutionary armed struggle to a call for immediate insurrection, without any preparatory political work amongst the masses. The insurrection, the guerilla struggle, is supposed to awaken the revolutionary potential of the masses immediately, by example. The theorisation and generalisation of the exceptional case of

Cuba are behind this conception. Comparisons with Vietnam do not apply. The objective conditions in Palestine have nothing in common with those in Vietnam — not only because of the geographical differences in the terrain, but because of the political conditions: two million Israelis, armed to the teeth, stand against only just the same number of Palestinians, half of whom are unarmed, and whose political maturity is still very inadequate. What was needed was the courage to envisage a long and multiform struggle. Instead the minority movements chose spectacular gestures, notably terrorist acts and the hijacking of aeroplanes which reached a peak in 1969-70. The lessons of the technical and political failures of this strategy have still not been drawn. On the contrary, this defeat led the minority groups to go on the offensive in Jordan in 1970, thus taking on responsibility for what followed. And while the execution of Wasfi Tall, in Cairo in November, in no way morally disturbs any Arab, it remains an act of desperation which sets the seal on a political *cul-de-sac*. These critiques do not mean that a 'front' strategy was necessary — but they do indicate that the childish impatience of the minority groups did objectively delay the maturation of the masses and weakened the Fatah, which is the only real mass organisation, however one may feel about it. The weaknesses and errors of the Fatah must doubtless carry their share of responsibility, if only for having created the conditions which facilitated the emergence of the minority movements and allowed the latter to take the unfortunate initiative of launching the offensive. Indeed the Fatah's self-criticism brings out this crucial point and makes it clear that revolutionaries have a place in its ranks. The critical analysis of the Palestinian movement's ideology (which is set out in Fouad Raouf's presentation[1]) enables one to understand the underlying reasons for these defeats.

The Zionist settlement in Palestine has deprived the Palestinian people of their country: only a minority of the people stayed in the occupied territories, while nearly two million Palestinians were packed into refugee camps in Jordan, Syria and Lebanon. These people, only the most fortunate of whom are proletarians (and only occasionally so at that) have no role in any permanent process of production. The ideology of their 'Return' which therefore inspires them, in conjunction with the continued prevalence of the old patriarchal relations and clientilist spirit of the petty chieftains (the Zaim), makes it impossible for them to conduct a real revolutionary war. The Fatah, whose fundamental constituency is the refugee social category, has not only failed to understand that the war of liberation is also a social war, it has reduced the former into a series of formulae dealing with armed struggle. Whilst it is quite true that the concrete conditions of the liberation struggle in Palestine are, as elsewhere, specific ones, it is nonetheless the case that whatever these conditions may be the liberation struggle can only succeed if it is also a social revolution; this is the *sine qua non* condition which allows the popular masses, led by the proletariat, to make that struggle their own and to give it an invincible strength, however strong the enemy may be. It is in this sense that the lessons of China, of Vietnam, of Cambodia and of Laos have a universal bearing. In the absence of this understanding, the leadership of the Palestinian movements has been *de facto* recaptured by the petty bourgeosie, which has imposed its conception of a front as being a mere amalgam, as opposed to an alliance of classes, each having its own autonomy, which it should be. The struggle is then reduced to its military dimension, which is not subordinated to the imperative need for the political development of popular social forces. As for the minority movements, especially the P.D.F.L.P., their support is drawn largely from the intellectual petty bourgeoisie which has been radicalised both in and out of the camps. But this category, divorced as it is from the impoverished masses, can of itself develop only a leftist ideology, 'as the *avant-garde* bearer of Marxist-Leninist knowledge.' In the occupied territories the peasant masses are still only a reserve of manpower for Israel. It is only to the extent that these masses will gradually be integrated as proletarians into the Israeli economy that the real revolutionary class, whose vocation it is to lead the struggle of the Palestinian people, will be constituted. Only the Palestinian proletariat can fulfil this role, especially since its bourgeoisie has disappeared, has gone off to integrate itself into the ruling classes of Jordan or to enrich itself by becoming the comprador bourgeoisie of the Gulf States.

The Return to Diplomacy, the Military Revenge of 1973 and its Consequences

In any case, the Palestinian drama certainly gave a renewed importance to the diplomatic scene. The United Nations' Jarring Mission, begun in January 1969, continued throughout 1970 and 1971 and was reinforced in November 1971 by the O.A.U.'s Senghor-Gowon-Ahidjo-Mobutu Mission. Negotiation now no longer concerned the Palestinians, it was an affair between states. Israel on the one hand, Egypt, Syria and Jordan on the other. The two superpowers were in agreement not only on the foundations but also on the form and stages of a gradual return to the *status quo ante*, based on the UN resolution of the 22nd November. For the moment, the organised Palestinians no longer constituted any serious obstacle. However, no solution emerged. The Arab people's opposition to a capitulation was very real especially in Syria and Egypt, but silent and unable, in the short term, to overthrow the equilibrium of forces. The provincialist demagogy which the Egyptian right was quick to use ('Let us abandon these Arabs who have caused us nothing but trouble, let us concentrate on our own Egyptian problems, etc.') found no echo amongst the Egyptian masses, but — partly thanks to the prevailing exhaustion — the regime did not feel itself threatened directly.

The obstacle — the only one, in fact — was Israel. Israel refused to act as was expected of it, refused to give up the Egyptian territories. For Israel is essentially annexationist. The idea of reuniting the Jews of the Diaspora makes territorial expansion essential. To give up the 'Law of Return', which is the basic pre-condition of a real solution to the problem, since only by the abolition of this law can a bi-ethnic (or bi-national) egalitarian secular democratic Palestine establish its human and geographical frontiers, (this is the Fatah's proposal), would have been to give up the Zionist vocation. There was thus no possible diplomatic solution apart from open capitulation: a peace treaty whereby Egypt, Syria and Jordan would give up the occupied territories to Israeli sovereignty.

On the contrary, the Israeli victory strengthened its most intransigent expansionists. Israel could hope to become the little 'major power' of the area, to substitute itself for the old colonial powers, to reduce the Arab states to a perpetual powerlessness, in brief to become the main bastion of imperialism, the dominant 'sub-imperialism' of the area.

This Israeli choice not only did away with the role of the Arab bourgeoisies of the area, it even ruined Sadat's attempts to solve, in his own way, Egypt's dramatic and urgent economic problems. Sadat's 'opening-up' programme was an attempt to create economic prosperity by calling in Western and Arab capital in order to satisfy the demands of a population exhausted by Nasserist state capitalism and the war. But as long as the Egyptian bourgeoisie was incapable of asserting itself at home and abroad, it could not convincingly attract foreign capital.

The 1973 War, conceived as a means to redress this situation, thus had precise and limited goals. Indeed Sadat handled its preparation, its course and its consequences in close co-operation with King Feisal. Feisal, for all his position at the head of Arab reaction, for all his fidelity to the class alliance with American imperialism, nonetheless also needed to redress the situation. For, parallel to the rise of an Israeli sub-imperialism, Iran's emerging pretensions to the same position were also making themselves felt. After the fall of Mossadegh and the destruction of the popular movement and its *avant-garde* — the Toudeh Party, a devotee of Moscow — the Shah took the initiative and instituted a modernisation from above: bourgeois agrarian reform, industrialisation based on oil income, creation of a powerful military force, etc. Faced with an Iran of 35 million people, Saudi Arabia and the Gulf States felt at a considerable disadvantage. At the end of 1972, the Shah had had his armies occupy the Arab islets of Tumb and Abu Musa, without even bothering to go through the usual diplomatic formulas to soothe Arab susceptibilities.

Sadat had little difficulty in convincing the Russians to supply arms — the USSR had no choice. The same was true of the defeated P.L.O., which no longer constituted an autonomous force. The active support of Algerian diplomacy, of a country which both headed the non-aligned countries, entertained good relations with Moscow and Peking, and was accepted by the West, was also forthcoming. That of President Ghadaffi was not even necessary.

The aims of the war were thus clearly defined: to re-establish Arab dignity, to obtain the restitution of Sinai and the Golan Heights through negotiation, to establish a little Arab Palestine independent of King Hussein, to definitely recognise in exchange a State of Israel reduced to its just proportions, and thus to impose the Arab bourgeoisie as the main voice in the dialogue with the United States and to put an end to Israel and Iran's ambitions to become the main sub-imperialisms. Military strategy was geared to these aims. And if Israel's attempt to foil this plan, by the Golan offensive which began on the 11th of October (the war had started on the 6th of October 1973) and then by surrounding the Egyptian Third Army at Suez on the eve of the cease-fire on the 25th of the same month, all came to nothing, it is quite simply because Kissinger and Brezhnev had already agreed, on the 20th October in Moscow, to bring Israel back to a more realistic view of things. Soviet-American differences only re-emerged later, when, satisfied with the immediate results of the war, the Arab bourgeoisie was quick — perhaps too quick — to 'thank' Moscow, or when Israel reassumed its previous attitude. The Geneva Conference which opened on the 20th November — as a concession to Syria and the USSR who had been left out of the Israelo-Egyptian disengagement agreement, signed on 18th January 1974, despite the anger of Algeria, Iraq and Libya — was to have no immediate outcome. Sadat opted for reinforcing the Washington-Cairo-Riyadh axis, received Nixon — who was about to resign due to the Watergate scandal — and made some tentative first steps towards Israel. Confidently, he awaited the reopening of the Suez Canal and the country's revival by means of an inflow of Arab and foreign capital.

The 1973 War certainly dispelled the myth of Israeli invincibility, both amongst the Arab masses and in Israel itself, where a new period began. The shock to Israeli morale at last made it possible for the population to face facts. After a quarter of a century of inebriation, Zionism entered a phase of decline. The victory re-established the internal credibility of the Arab bourgeoisie and, on the international level, the conjunction of the victory with the use of the oil weapon had convinced the United States to back the Arabs.

However, the balloons were soon pricked. Firstly, because Israel had still not given up. Two years after the October War there was not yet any question of the evacuation of the whole of the Sinai, still less of the Golan, just as there was no question of negotiating and accepting a Palestinian State administered by the P.L.P.. The threat of reopening the Geneva Conference was from then on a toothless one. Sadat had made too many concessions, too quickly. In June 1975 he accepted the reopening of the Canal without even recovering the Sinai passes in exchange. The September 1975 Israeli-Egyptian Agreement marked no significant progress. On the contrary, the installation of American technicians in the Sinai reduced Egypt's manoeuvring space to zero: by practically eliminating an eventual recourse to war, this installation puts Cairo at the mercy of Washington in all matters concerning an eventual Israeli retreat.

If Sadat accepted these conditions, it is simply because he believes in the imminence of a cascade of dollars. In fact the opening up of Egypt to foreign capital has had only one effect: the rapid enrichment of a few businessmen from the 'new class', and the further deterioration of the condition of the masses.

THE ERA OF RESTORATIONS: THE END OF NASSERISM, TOWARDS A RADICALISATION?

Did the defeat of June 1967, followed by the victory in 1973 sound the knell of Nasserism? What we can say for sure is that, in the short term, 1967 and 1973 facilitated a drift to the right: a reinforcement of the classical right-wing regimes, with Feisal cast as the hero, the Gulf Emirates as examples of success, and a newly self-confident King of Morocco; and also a restoration of the right in Egypt, in Syria, in Yemen, in the Sudan and in Tunisia. Faced with this drift, how good a fight will the few pockets of resistence (Algeria, Iraq, Libya) be able to put up; to what extent will the spark of radicalisation, as exemplified by South Yemen and Dhofar, spread further as the restoration of reaction leads deeper and deeper into dead-ends?

The Classical Arab Right: Second Wind or Swan-song?

Feisal, man of the moment. Who'd have thought it possible? When in 1958 Abdel Aziz Ibn Saud attempted, with help from Onassis, to get hold of a few oil tankers, a frown from Aramco was enough to make him drop the idea. Replaced by Faycal in 1958, Saud made a timid attempt at a come-back, basing himself on the rise of Nasserism; in 1960, Abdallah Tariqi, the first Arab Oil Minister, attempted to obtain some share in the fabulous flow of wealth. He failed. His allies were too weak: Prince Talal and the enlightened bourgeoisie of the Hejaz, who were the traditional opponents of the Wahabite princes of the Nedj, carried too little weight. But the Popular Union of the Arabian Peninsula, created by the Nasserists, was hardly more influential: an intervention here and there during the early Sixties, a few agreements with the Shammar tribes, were not enough to spoke the wheels of the man whom Nasser hated so much: by 1964 Faycal had definitely carried the day, and so, it seemed, had Aramco.

Until the Fifties, the companies of the famous Oil Cartel hardly bothered about the local ruling classes, not in Arabia, not in Venezuela, not in Iran or Iraq: secret inter-imperialist agreements, free concessions, merely symbolic royalties and gunboats were still the order of the day. There can be no doubt whatsoever that it was the Iranian people who put an end to the period of unlimited pillage. Defeat of the oil majors, however, still allowed for the fifty-fifty partition of profits which became prevalent during the Fifties. The partition was still highly unequal since the profits in question were based on artificial official prices. The progressive deterioration of these led the producer countries to form O.P.E.C. in 1960. For ten years the efforts of this organisation remained ineffective until, in 1970, circumstances enabled Libya to obtain better conditions. Algeria, which had been at the forefront of the struggle during the Sixties, was no longer alone. From 1972 onwards, the major offensive was launched, both on the level of prices and partition of profits on the one hand, and on the level of control, notably over the rate of exploitation, on the other. All the producers united: Iran (because of the Shah's growing hopes of setting up a sub-imperialism), Yankee Venezuela, neo-colonial Nigeria and Gabon, Algeria, Iraq, Libya, even Faycal's Arabia and the Gulf States. Conflicts of interest — between those producers whose reserves were limited and who sought to restrain production, and those whose resources were immense — were overcome. Control passed into the hands of the producer states who obtained majority shareholdings, in general of 60%, in those countries where the whole sector had not yet been nationalised, as it had already been in Algeria, Iraq or Libya. The West eventually accepted these conditions, and from then on its main concern was not to draw the maximum possible profit from the Black Gold, but to ensure a steady guaranteed supply. This guarantee was more or less forthcoming, if only because the profits, now retained by the local bourgeoisies, made for an increased integration into the world capitalist system, as the whole debate on the recycling of oil revenue has shown.

Nonetheless, the fact remains that the Arab bourgeoisie was effectively able to use the oil weapon, within the general framework of O.P.E.C., not only to reinforce its economic position but also as a political instrument. However much theatrics may have been mixed in with reality during the 'Oil War' — embargoes, cut-backs in production, etc. — the fact is that the Arab bourgeoisie got what it was after: Washington was forced to take it seriously. Faycal himself may well have paid for all this with his life: his assassination in 1975 is still shrouded in mystery, but the C.I.A. could quite well have had a part in it.

The prestige of oil, reinforced by that of Faycal, allowed the small Gulf States to bask in reflected glory. Until 1973 nobody paid much attention to these artificial states. Kuwait, formally independent since 1961, would have disappeared, absorbed by Kassem's Iraq, had it not been for the combination of protection by British paratroopers and Nasser's hostility towards his rival in Baghdad. Nobody is taken in by Kuwait's false democracy, where the non-autochthonous majority is deprived of all rights. As for the other states of the area, they were only granted independence by their British masters just before the oil crisis: in 1971. This was unproblematical in Qatar, where Emir Al Thani's Wahabite family had nothing to fear from anybody. The same was true in Abu Dhabi and in 'Trucial Oman': in 1966 the Intelligence Service hurriedly replaced the elderly and excessively backward Shakhbut in order to allow his brother Zaid to modernise the country, that is to say to facilitate the exploitation of its oil. The same operation was carried out in Muscat in 1970: the old Sultan, Said ben Taimur, made way for Kabbous. Oman, which hardly anybody remembered even as a British colony, became an independent state. Western journalists like to counterpose Bahrein's dynamism to the insignificance of the United Arab Emirates and Qatar. Quite possibly the island's society is more complex than that of the coast, and the country is less oil-rich. But there is hardly anything to marvel at in the fact that Emir Al Khalifa calls in foreign capital to exploit his cheap energy supply in the production, within his domains, of aluminium which is then exported. Neither on this level nor on that of democracy does Bahrein stand out as an example.

Faycal's rise and the new wealth of Arabia and the Gulf were to have distant echoes. The classical right felt itself revivified, not only in Cairo where from then on the Emirs were given the same princely welcome as in London, Nice or Los Angeles, but also in faraway Morocco and, closer to home, in Lebanon.

King Hassan II of Morocco, who in 1970 was still threatened by local Nasserism, managed to hold on to power. The failure of the attempt of July 1971, which followed the Marrakesh trial, further diminished the illusions of the petty bourgeois nationalist movement. The emboldened King then proceeded to liquidate his potential rival, Oufkir, and, to cap it all, managed to weld a national unity around himself from 1974 onwards over the question of the Spanish Sahara. Mauritania, a neo-colonial state from birth, had gradually moved closer to Algiers since 1972. But Algeria was to dissappoint Nouakchott by accepting the Spanish Sahara's claim to independence. The upshot came with the Madrid Agreement of November 1975, which handed two-thirds of the country to Morocco and one-third to Mauritania, thus completing the reconciliation between Nouakchott and Rabat.

In Lebanon, Pierre Gemayel's fascist phalanges, encouraged by the Palestinian defeats, went on the offensive in 1974 and 1975, and started hunting Palestinians in the streets of Beirut. Gradually the situation deteriorated into civil war. Whilst it was indeed a class war, it was nevertheless heavily mystified by religious conflicts. Today the Lebanese State which used to be dominated by one religious group no longer exists; a *de facto* partition has handed over a small Maronite Lebanon to the most reactionary forces, whilst in the South (with the help of the Palestinians) and in the North, a non-denominational popular alliance is in control. But will the latter be able to rebuild Lebanon on new foundations? The internal obstacles remain immense, aggravated as they are by the Israeli menace and by the role of the imperialists and their Arab allies. One can no longer keep quiet about the reactionary role played by Syria, whose primary concern has been to avoid a victory of the Lebanese left. What is being planned is nothing less than the final liquidation of the Palestinian movement, the smashing of its organisation, the P.L.O. and, if necessary, the dispersion of the population of the camps; in other words, a repetition in Lebanon of the operation carried out in Jordan during September 1970. The necessary conditions for the signature of a definitive peace with Israel are being met.

Egypt, Syria, Sudan, Yemen, Tunisia: the Era of Restorations

In Egypt, Gamal Abdel Nasser's death in September 1970 accelerated a process begun in 1967. The previous mere drift to the right became more like a brutal change of direction, both in terms of external alliances and in terms of internal orientations. In May 1971, the main core of the Nasserist ruling group was charged with conspiracy and arrested, including Vice-President Ali Sabri, General Mohamed Fawzi and the old Ministers and Chiefs of Police, notably Shaarawi Gomaa and Sami Charaf. At the same time, President Sadat rehabilitated many agents and politicians of the old regime who were known for their pro-American sympathies, such as the Amin brothers, as well as corrupt businessmen and big landlords who had attempted to resist the agrarian reforms. Key positions of power were found for all of these.

Sadat's foreign policy liquidated Egypt's alliance with the Soviets; he proclaimed his faith in Kissinger, visited the United States and received Nixon with great pomp, openly abandoned Arab solidarity in order to negotiate directly with Israel under American auspices, etc. His home policy consisted in the announcement of a new era, the so-called 'opening up' (*infitah*); in other words, economic liberalisation. The private sector was encouraged and quickly seized opportunities in every area where the superprofits of speculation could be made thanks to emerging inflation, notably in commerce, building and property. The sharing out of the public sector was officially proposed.

From 1973 onwards the new Hegazi Government and that of Mamdouh Salem which followed in 1974 took steps in this direction. A series of laws and decrees in 1974 and 1975 exempted foreign investments from taxes for 5 years, opened the Canal Zone as a free trade area, authorised foreign merchant banks to sidestep the currency exchange regulations, re-established private importation, dismantled the public sector's control bodies, allowed public companies to operate competitively, invited businessmen to participate in their administration, limited the power of workers' representatives, and finally put part of the public companies' shares up for sale. The agrarian reform was under attack too: in June 1975 an amendment put rents up by 25%, authorised owners to evict tenants who fell into arrears and entrusted to tribunals the arbitration of disputes which until then had fallen under the jurisdiction of rural committees which had been more closely linked with the peasants.

The new authorities based all their hopes on a massive flow of American aid and Arab oil money, as the means to overcome at least the short-term problems. It therefore set out to offer foreign and local capital the maximum possible economic and political guarantees. But these concessions did not reassure Arab capital, nor did they convince the United States to make a special effort. For the working class, the people as a whole, and even to some extent the class which had benefited from the Nasserist system, were totally opposed to the dismantling of the public sector, just as the peasants who had benefited from the agrarian reform were opposed to the new laws; all this made any return to the old system very difficult. A series of strikes at Helouan and Mahalla-El-Kobra had to be put down violently in September 1974, and again in January and March 1975; meanwhile the Communist Party was reconstituting itself. The farce of the 'tributes' (*manaber*) which were supposed to guarantee some degree of freedom of expression for all the different political currents, including the extreme left, was quickly exposed; the operation could hardly camouflage the full-blown return to the fore of the right-wing pro-imperialist press. At the same time the resignation of Mohamed Hassanein Heykal, an old confidant of Nasser's, from the paper El Ahram, signalled, despite the man's dubious past, the open break with Nasserism. An interim plan (1974-75) was to have re-established the pre-conditions of prosperity. It failed: the expected foreign aid, £1,100 million, did not all arrive (only £450 million was received), inflation increased, the balance of trade deficit went from £200 million in 1972 to more than £1,300 million in 1975. The contrast between the growing misery of the people and the enrichment of a small group of business operators grew apace.

It was the ambiguous and contradictory choices of Nasserism which had created the pre-conditions for inflation and these inequalities. Its bureaucratic style reinforced a class, a part of which eventually revealed itself as openly reactionary. The liquidation of the popular organisations facilitated the transfer of power. Right from the middle of the Sixties it was obvious to the more lucid communists that the modernisation and industrialisation strategy could lead only to bankruptcy, that the failure of the five year plan, the emerging inflation and the fragility of foreign dependence represented not just marginal errors but the objective limits imposed by the regime's class nature.

In Syria the main achievements of state capitalism were not immediately threatened. Nevertheless, a definite shift to the right had taken place. The Atassi regime had tolerated a left-wing pressure group in its midst, which had pushed the country to go beyond state capitalism. In 1970 the right wing of the Baath carried out a coup which overthrew the regime. General Hafez el Assad, who has since then presided over the country's fate, had the whole of the old Baathist left wing arrested, including President Atassi and Ibrahim Makhos; he also put an end to the activities of the Palestinians. However, his main concern was to stop the movement of change, not to reverse it completely. On this level he was probably even less of a free agent than Sadat: Israel threatens his country even more than it threatens Egypt.

In the Sudan, on the other hand, the battle between the old imperialist forms of domination and those of emergent state capitalism is not yet over. Following the 1969 coup, which brought General Gafar el Numeri to power, the new regime had been forced to handle the communists gently. In March 1970, following an attempted right-wing coup led by the feudalists of the old regime, notably the powerful chieftains of the Ansar fraternity, the Government's survival had been entirely due to the support afforded by the communists. But, reinforced by this victory, the regime then decided to attack its own left: in February 1971 the Communist Party was outlawed, and in May a one-party system was proclaimed. Thrown off course by this development, certain elements of the popular movement (communists, trade unionists, intellectuals and students) attempted a military coup in July 1971. The coup's failure was followed by thousands of arrests and the hanging of leaders (in particular, that of the communist leader A.K. Mahgoub). The roles played in this sad story by Ghadaffi — who handed over to Khartoum the passengers of the plane carrying the leaders of the Sudanese left — and by Sadat were crucial. The regime has become the prisoner of the old right wing and no longer seeks to impose the goals of state capitalism proper.

In North Yemen, the Nasserists have managed to pull off the spectacular stunt of bringing the country back to its starting point. Up to the death of Imam Ahmad in 1962, politics in Yemen consisted of the hostility of the Sunni (Shafei) commercial bourgeoisie of the coast towards Imam Zeidi and the inland Sheikhs who ruled over a peasantry cut off from the rest of the world. When Ahmad died, the coup led by the republican and Nasserist General Al Sallal, which eliminated Ahmad's son Badr immediately, could have heralded a new era. But, by refusing to base themselves on the exploited peasants, by choosing an alliance with the coastal bourgeoisie, Sallal and Nasser played into the hands of the forces of reaction. The long Egyptian military intervention (1962-67) having failed, that is to say having facilitated Badr's counter-attack supported by Faycal, Egypt was forced to withdraw after its defeat in 1967. The local left, which the Nasserists had opposed, did not manage to take over; its emergence, during Badr's seige of Sanaa in February 1968 was short-lived. What followed was nothing less than a restoration, plain and simple: behind a republican facade, Faycal imposed a satellisation process, which was welcomed by the bourgeoisie which felt threatened by the radicalisation in South Yemen.

Tunisia, the Lebanon of the West, has also experienced a right-wing restoration in keeping with its socialism. Local Nasserism had been of the vintage which blended the proclamation of the *'Combattant Supreme'* with Ahmad Ben Salah's pro-American 'socialism'. The latter was eliminated in September 1969 and today it is the Nouira Cabinet which handles current affairs. Each passing day, however, allows the comprador bourgeoisie to gnaw away at the few gains which the bureaucrats have made.

Algeria, Iraq, Libya, South Yemen: a belated Nasserism or something better?

It can truly be said that all the objective conditions conspired to move Algeria to the left: from the popular origins of the F.L.N., to the complex of circumstances which dominated the situation at the time of independence. The fact that the *Pieds Noirs* had deserted the agricultural export sector of the economy which they had previously clung to made it possible for peasant demands to be clearly expressed: similarly, their parallel desertion of the small urban enterprises opened up possibilities of workers' self-management which existed nowhere else in the Arab world. Simultaneously, the Algerian State inherited the strategic positions which France had taken over during the years preceding independence. The French State had even controlled the oil sector, which it had developed as a means of reinforcing its autonomy vis-a-vis the American companies which dominated the Cartel. France had also taken the initiative, within the framework of the Constantine Plan, of filling the gap created by the absence of private capital and starting a rapid, if dependent, industrialisation of Algeria. Gradually, during the Sixties, the Algerian State consolidated its position by systematic nationalisations carried out mainly from 1966 to 1971, and by setting up strict means of control over the private sector (regulations affecting currency exchange, prices, supply, etc.). At the same time, the State extended its powers at the expense of self-management in agriculture and in small enterprises. The development strategy based on this framework was supposed to rapidly industrialise the country by setting up powerful modern units, both in the base sector ('industrialisation industries' was the official term) and in the consumer sector. However, as these installations progressed, thanks to capital derived from oil, new forms of dependence emerged to replace the old colonial forms. The distortions inherited from the past — especially the backwardness of the agricultural sector — limited the internal market and imposed the necessity of a programme of industrial exportation. Imported technology proved too expensive and too quickly outdated, for Algeria to appropriate it directly — but because of the dependence on foreign outlets, such technology became essential.[4]

The contradictions which broke the Nasserist regime soon developed in Algeria as well: bureaucratisation, passivity of the masses, failure to build a popular party, intimate linkage between the new class and foreign capital, etc. The relative abundance of financial resources facilitated this process of development in the framework of the new unequal international division of labour which replaced the old model. However, it also accentuated the new model's characteristics.[5]

Nonetheless, the fact remains that the international situation which provides the context for Algerian evolution is different from that which was faced by Nasser's Egypt. The latter was directly confronted with Zionism, was thrown into the general struggle over Arab leadership, the battle of the superpowers for the area. The Algerian phenomenon, in contrast, appeared at a time when the imperialist system was beginning to face a crisis and when the contradictions which put the Third World in an opposition to the imperialist centres were growing more acute, whilst those between the US and the USSR were dying down. The old non-alignment — Nasser's and Tito's — was, as its name indicates, a refusal to integrate into one or other of the two politico-military blocs. Today's non-alignment, of which Algeria has become the leading light, has become synonymous with the struggle for the Third World's economic independence.

In fact, the F.L.N.'s populist origins have not yet finished making themselves felt within Algeria itself. If the contradictions of the strategy of integration into the new international division of labour become sharper, this latent populism may flourish again. The spark of 'agrarian revolution' lit by Boumedienne bears witness to the liveliness of this populism, a liveliness that the cultural contradictions specific to Algeria accentuate. After having been perverted by French colonisation, independent Algeria set out to re-Arabise itself. But this choice was contradictory to the choice made concerning the form of development. An education policy based on the Arab language in schools would have meant a slow development, from the foundations and starting in the countryside. The quickest way to train a skilled urban and proletarianised work-force was by an education policy based on French. The latter policy, incidentally, has already been spectacularly successful, far more so than under French colonisation. Contradictions such as this one, of which Boumedienne is quite aware, may eventually cause some re-evaluation of the sort of development which has been pursued till now.

Of all the local species, it is definitely Iraqi Nasserism which contains the most diverse strains. True, General Aref's replacement in July 1968 by General Ahmed el Bakr, brought about no immediate change in the prevailing system. And quite probably, it is in terms of Baghdad's hostility to Cairo at the time that one can best explain Baghdad's support for the left-wing Sudanese putschists. Nonetheless, demagogy eventually had to make way for a more coherent set of formulations, especially as Hussein Sadam's position grew firmer, with the support of the whole of the left, including the left-wing of the Baath, the Communist Party and the Kurdish Democratic Party. The Iraqi Party, the only survivor of the old Arab communist parties, may have adopted many revisionist theses, but it never completely lost its anchorage in the proletariat.

But all this amounted to little more than political mouthings. The development strategy remained that of state capitalism, in no way distinguishable in this respect from the one that went bankrupt in Nasser's Egypt. No solution had been found to the Kurd problem, which will have to wait for the development of genuine popular power in all the areas of the country.

In Libya, the Ghadaffi regime which came to power in September 1969 has stayed true to itself, despite the eclipse of its leading light. For all his outrageous anti-imperialist declarations, Ghadaffi remained a Muslim, a fundamentalist and an anti-communist: he played an important role in the reactionary Khartoum coup. His nationalism could have appealed to the Egyptian popular masses, but instead his traditionalism soon became the butt of their sarcasm.

To this picture of the remnants of Nasserism, one must counterpose the gleam of hope appearing in Southern Arabia. Once again it is a particularly poor and backward country which shows the way. Southern Arabia, once a prosperous region, has been miserably poor for centuries: Aden, which had 100,000 inhabitants in the 13th century, lost its function when the Portuguese established direct links between Europe, West Africa and Asia; it had become a village of 500 inhabitants when the British seized it in 1839. Muscat, which had ruled over an important maritime empire and in 1850 still counted 55,000 souls, had rapidly become depopulated after the fall of that empire, so that in 1870 it had only 8,000 inhabitants. The Sunni bourgeoisie of the coast did not even manage to revive during Aden's colonial development: the essential fractions of the new comprador bourgeoisie were imported from India by the British, thereby relegating the local *shaffei* to subordinate positions. Minority peasant communities survived in the interior, as in so many areas of the Arab world: the remains of Qarmate societies, of Himyari communities in Dhofar, of Ibadite mountain peoples in Oman. The Colonial Office imposed the rule of cruel and odious tinpot Sultans. After 1956, when Britain decided to withdraw East of Suez and to turn Aden into a major base, there seemed no problem in setting up a Federation dominated by British sponsored Sultans. There was no reason to expect any serious trouble: in Oman the uprising of Imam Ghaleb against the Sultan of Muscat in 1957-59 remained firmly within the framework of traditional politics and was soon taken over as part of the prolongation of conflict between British and American oil interests who were quarrelling, each through their own Sheikhs, over the Oasis of Buraimi. In Aden the bourgeois Nahda movement, inspired by Nasserism, posed no real threat, for all its appeals to Yemeni unity and its hostility to the Sultans.

Neither the Intelligence Service, nor the Egyptian *moukhabarate*, nor *a fortiori* the C.I.A., had supposed that the peasants of the interior were capable of supplying an answer to the problems of the contemporary Arab

world. The formal creation of the Federation in 1962 coincided with the
generalised revolt of these 'backward' peasants. Yet, right from the start,
the South Yemen National Liberation Front had proclaimed its aims. It
opened fire right from 1964, to signal to these peasants that the time had
come for revenge, after so many decades. The more hesitant elements,
still struck by the glory of Nasserism, split off in 1965, to create the
O.S.Y.L.F. (Occupied South Yemen Liberation Front), led by Al Asnag and
Makawi and hostile to the guerilla war. This allowed the F.L.N. to become
even more radical, despite the refusal of its leader, Qahtan al Shaabi, to
break with the Nasserists. The majority, led by Mohsen Ibrahim and
Abdallah Khamri, proved capable of continuing alone, of beating the
Sultans and of presenting the British with a *fait accompli* on Independence
Day, the 30th November 1967.

The Popular Republic of South Yemen had not finished with its
problems. On the contrary, it was only just beginning to grasp their true
nature. The collapse of Aden's parasitical economy following the closure
of the Suez Canal no doubt finally helped South Yemen to discover the
Maoist formula which stresses self-reliance. In March 1968, once Qahtan
had been removed, the left-wing group led by Abdel Fatah Ismail, Salem
Robea Ali and Ali Nasser could open a new chapter in Arab history: the
construction of a workers' and peasants' party having as its goal a long self-
reliant transition, the pre-condition of an eventual true socialism.

In the Sultanate of Oman, the British were also having serious difficulties.
Sultan Kabbous, as reactionary as his backward predecessor despite an
affected modernism, could not put down the rebellion in Dhofar. This
rebellion, which had begun in 1963, could well have turned out to be
nothing more than an episode of regionalist opposition. Gradually, it turned
into a radical challenge to the feudal and capitalist exploitation of the
peasants of Dhofar. Imperialism was responding to a real threat when it
organised the joint Anglo-Iranian military intervention, with Faycal and
Sadat busily isolating the revolutionaries on the political and diplomatic
level. Cut off from the rest of the world, abandoned by the Nasserists,
betrayed by the revisionists, the revolutionaries of Dhofar continue to wage
an exemplary, if desperate struggle.

5

SOME CONCLUSIONS
AND PROBLEMS

THE HISTORY OF THE ARAB WORLD AND THE
NATIONAL QUESTION

We must now pose the question of nationhood in new terms. The mystical and mysterious basis for nationhood proposed by bourgeois science gets us nowhere, and neither does Stalin's reduction of this social reality to the modern capitalist world. On the contrary, the history of the Arab world gives specific scientific contours to the concept of nationhood, which tie in with the general hypothesis of *Unequal Development*. The propositions concerning the definition of this social fact which we call nationhood lead to the following formulations. Firstly, the nation is a social phenomenon which can appear at every stage of history: it is not necessarily and exclusively a correlate of the capitalist mode of production. Secondly, the nation appears when there exist not only the elementary conditions of geographical contiguity, reinforced by the use of a common language (which does not exclude variants of dialect), but also a social class which controls the central state apparatus and ensures economic unity in the life of the community: this class need not necessarily be the capitalist national bourgeoisie. Thirdly, the phenomenon of nationhood is a reversible process: it can develop and grow stronger or, on the contrary, it can weaken and fade away, according to whether the social class in question reinforces its unificatory power or loses it altogether. In the latter case the society can regress into a formless conglomeration of more or less related ethnic groups. These ethnic groups can re-form as one or more nations if history again allows a social class to fulfil the unificatory functions which allow one to distinguish between a nation and an ethnic group.

If applied to Arab history, these theoretical formulations shed a great deal of light on the contradictory aspects of the national question in this part of the world. In this sense the Arab world has only been a nation during short periods of its history; on the other hand, some, but not all, of its constituent regions were already nations when they were Arabised (Egypt, for example). After the decline of the Arab nation, some regions became autonomous nations, whilst others did not attain this national stage and remained conglomerates of ethnic groups. The social class which undertook Arab national unification was that of the merchant-warriors.

Indeed, the social formations of the pre-colonial Arab world were not feudal but commercial, that is to say that the main surplus on which the imperial state, the civilisation and the material life of its ruling classes were based was not mainly drawn from the agricultural product of the local peasants, but from the profits of long distance trade. Let us be quite clear: the issue is not that of the origin of the state but rather of the nature of that state during the imperial stages of its centuries of greatness.

A series of major historical events brought about national regression: the Crusades and the shifting of the commercial centre of gravity from the Arab to the Italian cities, the fall of Baghdad under the assault of the Mongols in the 13th century, then the Ottoman conquest in the 16th, the shift of Mediterranean trade to the Atlantic during the same period, and consequently the direct link Europe established with Eastern Asia and Black Africa, thereby depriving the Arabs of their traditional role of intermediary.

The disappearance of the Arab nation gave new life to other nations. Because the Egyptian oasis constitutes a peasant formation, Egypt has always retained a certain autonomy, even during the Arab nation's greatest period. And when the Arab world as a whole lost its nationhood and became a conglomerate of peoples during the 13th and 14th centuries, Egypt asserted itself again as an autonomous nation.

The social class which undertook this renaissance was not that of the merchant-warriors but the landowning bureaucratic aristocracy. Under Ali Bey in the 18th century, and especially under Mohamed Ali in the 19th, this class gave a national character back to Egypt, a character which was something more than a mere geographical reality. The other attempts at constituting a nation — notably those in Morocco, in Tunisia, in Algeria under Abdel Kader, in the Sudan with Mahdism, in Yemen and in Lebanon — were not very far-reaching, not only because in some cases they fell prey to foreign attacks (for example in Algeria and the Sudan) but also and especially because the level of development of the local (agricultural) productive forces was not sufficient to ensure a surplus sufficient to establish the class which attempted to build up the nation. The fate of the dominant class was thus dependent mainly on its ability to draw on foreign surplus through international trade, and consequently was never independent of circumstances external to the society. These attempts at nationhood therefore remained embryonic and unfinished, whilst in Egypt a thousand year old nation, whose fate was not tied to foreign relations, was reborn. In Syria and Iraq, where Arab feeling has always been lively, the attempts at throwing off the Ottoman yoke in the 19th century were incomparably weaker than in Egypt: the Syrian commercial class, which was once so flourishing, had become feeble, the landowning bureaucratic aristocracy was impoverished by the return of the desert in Mesopotamia, and the peasantry was locked in by the closed horizons of its isolated mountain strongholds.

Egypt attempted to rebuild the Arab nation around itself. This was the real meaning of Mohamed Ali and Ibrahim Pacha's military conquests. The programme's abrupt interruption in 1840, then the military defeat by the English in 1882 put a stop to this attempt. Egypt carried on as a nation, but as an oppressed nation.

With the integration of the Arab world into the capitalist system, as a dominated and oppressed region, do we see the birth of a new social class which could pretend to national hegemony, that is to say could unify the economy and centralise power? And what would be the context of such unification: individual states or the Arab whole? The vicissitudes of the internal politics of the various states, particularly of Egypt, Iraq and Syria from the 1920's onwards, prove that the new (latifundist and commercial) bourgeoisie engendered by integration into the capitalist system could not pretend to this hegemony, neither in terms of the various states, no *a fortiori*, in terms of the Arab world as a whole.

Indeed this class was not the one which ensured the economic and political unity of the country. Those functions were fulfilled by the dominant imperialism of which this class is nothing but the appendage. The weakness of this class is thus that of the Arab (Egyptian, Syrian, Iraqi) nations and of the Arab 'nation'. The first Palestinian War (1948) drove the point home. It was not the implacable power of Zionism's penetration which opened up the possibility of Israel's establishment; rather it was the weakness of the Arab nations (or nation).

The new social classes which took over from the latifundist and commercial bourgeoisie following the defeat of 1948 were not noticeably more capable of assuming a real national hegemony, either in terms of particular states or in terms of the Arab area as a whole. Indeed state capitalism replaced latifundist and commercial capitalism by three sets of measures: firstly, an agrarian reform which replaced the old aristocracy with a class of kulaks, thereby widening the internal market; secondly, a programme of public nationalisations which expropriated both the dominant foreign capital and the big local bourgeoisie associated with it; thirdly, a programme of public industrialisation made possible by the wider market created by the first two measures. A set of measures of this kind does not necessarily constitute a stage of transition towards socialism. For that to be the case, these measures would have to be associated with an effective form of popular power and a proletarian ideology. Then, and only then, does agrarian reform become a first step towards the mobilisation of the whole of the peasantry, especially the poorest (and most numerous) layers of the latter, and not an end in itself which must be stabilised as soon as kulakisation is completed. Then, and only then, are planned industrialisation and development of agriculture not based either on the partial widening of the market made possible by kulakisation or simply on the transfer to the state of profits which until then were appropriated by foreign capital and its associated private local capital (it is this transfer which establishes the economic base of the new bureaucracy). Failing the above, the model of accumulation described is in every way analogous to that of capitalist accumulation, and can hardly be called socialism, since it leaves the masses outside its system. It is then just development for a minority, albeit a widened one; a minority made up of the class of kulaks and of the bureaucracy, which has become a state bourgeoisie. But this programme offers no development to the broad masses. It is thus incapable of really mobilising the latter, of constituting itself by their democratically organised every-day will. One could invoke the Western bourgeoisie revolution as evidence of the possibility of a capitalist road to development which excluded the masses. But to do so would be to assume that history can repeat itself, to forget the subtle transformations which imperialism has brought about. Integration into the imperialist system has already created a specific situation different to that which characterised today's advanced capitalist countries when they were going through their industrial revolution. In the Third World integration has proletarianised and impoverished the broad masses, without managing to integrate them into the system of capitalist accumulation: there has been no extension of wage-labour keeping pace with the disintegration of pre-capitalist society; there has been no constant improvement in wages; integration failed to achieve all this in the Third World precisely because of domination by an already existing imperialist system. This is the sense in which the capitalist road is closed and in which socialism is an objective necessity in the underdeveloped countries. The fact that it was not the proletariat which exercised hegemony during the changeover in the Arab world removes any possibility of statist rule being a possible transition to socialism. From then on, the new state capitalism, which benefits only a minority of the new classes, must accept that it will remain trailing along in the wake of a system which dominates the world. This dependence, renewed and deepened in comparison with that of the old latifundist and commercial bourgeoisie, manifests itself at all levels: that of technological dependence, that of the privileged classes' pattern of consumption, and that of their ideology.

Is Arab nationalism doomed to failure? Is the Arab nation condemned to remain a chimera? In fact, the negative reveals the positive: the very incapacities of the dependent state bourgeoisie reveal the necessity for a proletarian outcome. But how does nationalism figure in all this?

Not all the social formations known to history necessarily imply a nation; it is only those which are based on a mode of production which demands a centralisation of political power and economic organisation which do so. The formations of feudal Europe are typical examples of cases where the absence of political and economic centralisation reduces an ethnic group (be it Germanic or Italian or French) to a non-national conglomerate of regions. On the other hand, the formations of ancient Egypt and China, where centralisation was essential to the major works which had to be undertaken, were able to create nations. The formations based on a developed trade have also often engendered nations, as is borne out by the case of ancient Greece (despite the absence of a centralised political authority) or by that of the Arab world. Similarly, in Europe, when the absolutist monarchies united territories into nations, they had to base themselves on the merchants of the mercantilist period; the examples of England and France are typical.

The capitalist mode of production brings about a level of nationhood which is far more intense than those which existed in pre-capitalist social formations, because the centralisation of economic power is itself greatly intensified by the creation of an internal market for labour, capital and merchandise. This doubtless explains why Marxists have tended to think of the phenomenon of nationhood as a concomitant of capitalism — especially since in Europe the old pre-capitalist society, feudal society, had not been a national one.

The Third World's necessary transition to socialism will also have to create this internal market — but not in the forms, or with the content, of the capitalist market: this difference, according to our analysis, is precisely the one which separates state collectivism from socialism. Nonetheless this market must be capable of integrating people, of integrating them more fully than that of a Third World capitalism which can only be dependent, and thus limited, state capitalism. The vehicle for this integration, for its proletarian content, remains the nation: a nation of proletarians (as opposed to a proletarian nation). To the Trotskyists, socialism is purity and nationalism a deviation. In fact, in real social terms, both Vietnam and China demonstrate the existence of a proletarian nationalism. They even show that proletarian nationalism is the only kind which still has the strength which bourgeois nationalism once had, and that the only socialist revolutions of our time take place where nationalism does not figure as an autonomous tendency which is juxtaposed, albeit allied to, socialism, but where socialism is also nationalism. In a word which capitalism has unified and yet stratified, the oppression of the proletariat and the proletarianised masses of the dominated periphery is not just social oppression, it is also national oppression. The complete fusion of socialism and nationalism then becomes the pre-condition for the liberation of oppressed peoples. Were this liberation to be generalised, it would close one chapter of history and open another: that of the transcendence of nations in a socialist universe.

The necessary and possible national hegemony of the proletariat, in a revolution which is both national and social is one thing, and nationalism as an ideology is quite another. Nationalism as an ideology expresses the hegemony of the petty bourgeoisie, the effective domination of the movement by this class. There is no historical inevitability about this. The strength of the petty bourgeoisie is tailored to the weaknesses of the proletariat.

In the last analysis it is thus Arab communism, in its weaknesses which is responsible for petty bourgeois hegemony. The fact that communism in the Arab world originally developed in petty bourgeois circles is neither an anomaly (it happens this way as a rule in the Third World) nor a latent vice. But Arab communism could not move beyond this stage without a correct theory. And a correct theory is one which understands that only the proletariat can liberate a country oppressed by imperialism, and that the revolution must be led by that proletariat. Correct theory grasps that while that revolution's first task is to bring about democratic change, this is not a stage which is distinguishable by the class nature of the powers that carry it out from the next stage, socialist revolution. This is the true lesson of China and Indochina. Instead, Arab communism eventually accepted, although not without reticence, a theory and a practice which in the last analysis was a theory of stages, a theory which either straight-forwardly allowed the petty bourgeoisie to retain its leadership of the national stage, or — which amounts to much the same thing — accepted placing the party of the proletariat under the petty bourgeois banner. Communist and nationalist petty bourgeois thus came to lose their distinct visions of the future, and were reduced to the same common denominator, state socialism. The revisionist conception of Marxism necessarily had to lead to such an outcome. It is only now that the Arab communists are beginning to develop the first elements of a critical analysis of the situation. But an analysis, however correct, is not enough. Without a revolutionary practice, theory is condemned to degenerate. What is needed today is a break with petty bourgeois circles, with their lifestyles and with their limited forms of political action, in order to undertake another kind of action, amongst the proletarianised and popular masses, especially the rural ones. In this case, practice is more important than theory, for a fundamen-tally correct practice (action within the struggle of the revolutionary classes which are the motor of history) helps in the re-evaluation of partially false theory — but this does not work the other way round. Were it to break with revisionism, Arab communism could implant itself amongst the proletarian and pauperised masses of the Arab world. This communism's nature would necessarily change, for it would then have to assimilate itself to the history of its people, their culture and their traditions (as happened in East Asia), in order to discover the road towards socialist revolution. It would cease to be a foreign ideology superimposed on a national reality, an avatar of European history and of Europe's domination over the Arab world. It would finally become capable of settling national problems, both political and cultural, and the problems of the socialist transformation of society.

THE QUESTION OF FEUDALISM IN THE ARAB WORLD AND THE FAILURE OF ARAB MERCANTILISM

The Unequal Development Thesis

According to our 'unequal development' thesis, when a mode of production is necessarily overtaken by a more evolved mode which allows for greater development of the productive forces, this takes place not in the centre of the first mode, not in those societies where that mode is most firmly established and effective, but on its periphery, amongst the weak links of the system; in other words amongst the less advanced societies where that mode is less firmly established.

This thesis of ours contrasts with a vision which we shall call both mechanistic and linear, which attributes a universal character to a supposed succession of five modes of production (primitive communism, slavery, feudalism, capitalism, socialism). This latter thesis admits that it is possible for backward societies to accelerate and even to jump a stage of the general evolution. But it does not conceive of the possibility that a superior stage could actually be initiated and flourish first in a more backward society. Europe's move from barbarism to feudalism, skipping over the stage of slave society, has been explained in such terms. As for the Russian Revolution, which took place in a relatively backward country, Stalin supported the idea of 'socialism in one country' without worrying too much about the theoretical implications of this conclusion for historical materialism; Trotsky, on the other hand, believed that the fate of socialism depended on revolution in the advanced countries.

The unequal development thesis recognises that history has a meaning, and, in the last analysis, attributes the general direction of historical movement to the development of the productive forces. Neither capitalism nor socialism are the products of chance. The pre-capitalist relations of production had to be overthrown and capitalist relations of production established, thus making it possible for the productive forces to leap forwards, which then in its turn made it necessary to establish socialist relations of production. But this thesis does *not* admit that, from this, one can deduce the necessity of a universal model of evolution which would supposedly impose itself everywhere by some process of destiny.

Dominant pre-bourgeois social thought did not attempt to explain the history of humanity; the very idea of evolution was unknown, and thinkers thus set about justifying an established order, considered as eternal, in terms which were religious and generally specific to a given society. There were, it is true, occasional remarkable outbreaks of lucidity in this long history of human thought; but such occurrences, in Greece or amongst men such as Ibn Khaldoun, are hardly characteristic of the essence of pre-bourgeois ideology.

Bourgeois social thought grew up in opposition to this static ideology:

it sought to account for the constant movement of transformation which the permanent revolution of the productive forces introduces into capitalism, but it sought to account for them in absolute terms so that capitalism appeared as the realisation in itself of Reason. Thus the Enlightenment confused the laws of social evolution with those of nature. Later, analogies were established between the Darwinian laws of the evolution of species and the laws of competition. There was a great pretence that social laws apply to society in the same way as physical laws apply to nature. Furthermore, because this thought was stamped by its Eurocentric character, it tended to offer the history of Europe as the model *par excellence* of universal history. Bourgeois social thought is thus *at best* Eurocentric, materialist, mechanistic and linear. At best — since hardly had the capitalist order been established than already it had to mobilise the same old theological and static pre-bourgeois arguments in order to deny the socialist and proletarian critique which its rule had given birth to. The evolution of economic thought, from the classical school to vulgar economy, bears this out. Furthermore, the direct domination of the economic relations particular to the capitalist mode of production was to give bourgeois ideology its essential content: economicism. Within this general philosophical framework, technology became an autonomous *primus movens*, stemming from the 'progress of the human spirit', the secular version of God in Enlightenment thought.

Marxism developed both as a continuation of Enlightenment thought and as a counterpoint. Its analysis of alienation enabled it to grasp the specificity of social as opposed to natural laws; and to do so it produced an arsenal of scientific concepts: 'productive forces', 'relations of production', 'economic base', 'ideological superstructure', 'mode of production', etc. Although these concepts were forged in the Western proletariat's struggle against capitalist exploitation, in other words on the basis of European history (which it enables one to interpret correctly), they have a universal value which allows Marxism to transcend Eurocentrism.

However, things did not stop there. Not only did bourgeois ideology continue to exert pressure on the working class movement, (the dominant ideology of any society being the ideology of its ruling class), but from the turn of the century onwards, imperialism created conditions favourable to a political recapture of the working class in the centre, a reintegration of Marxism into bourgeois thought. A vulgar Marxism grew up under these conditions, absorbing the Eurocentrism, the economicism, the linear and mechanistic vision of bourgeois ideology. This vulgar Marxism has indeed occasionally discovered certain expressions and usages which give rise to ambiguity, even in the writings of Marx and Engels. For Marxism had to assert itself against the resurgent vestiges of pre-bourgeois ideologies, and could only base itself on the known history of its time, that is European history: for example Engel's unfortunate attempt at a 'dialectic of nature' betrays the persistent influence of positivist scientism. Bolshevism itself, for all that it grew up as an opposition to the open treason of the Second International's revisionism, nonetheless also belonged to this period in the history of the working class movement. Whilst it was able to break away categorically from the political strategy of revisionism, it did continue to express points of view — notably those put forward by Kautsky — which are at the root of the economicist deviations. It is essential to break away completely from any religious appreciation of Marxism, to accept that this living body of thought — the product of working class struggles — is not protected from error by any texts, however important, which would supposedly constitute a finished product making the contribution of later struggles irrelevant. These steps backward, these bourgeois revisions of Marxism, must constantly be unearthed and exposed, for the tendency to interpret historical materialism as the unilateral determination of a social evolution based on the autonomous development of the productive forces is unfortunately still with us. The constant use of the adjective 'dialectical' is never enough to change the real nature of an analysis.

The essence of our thesis is that the tributary mode is the most general form of pre-capitalist class society; that slavery is the exception not the rule, and that, like the pure merchant mode, it is marginal; that feudalism is a peripheral form of the tributary mode and that, precisely because it was an immature form still stamped by characteristics of its original communal society, it was fated to transcend itself more easily, thereby ensuring Europe's particular destiny. Let us dwell briefly on each of these points.

The tributary mode defines both relations of domination (state governing class and governed peasants) and relations of exploitation (extortion of surplus in the form of tribute). The transparency of these relations of exploitation implies that relations of domination dominate the society, that the key dimension ideologised in the society is the political one. Such a mode, in its mature form, is very stable. It can thus absorb developments in the means of production without bringing into question the relations of production (the set of relations of domination and exploitation). This should remind us that the thesis which argues that the relations of production are mechanically determined by the level of development of the means of production is not a Marxist thesis but a product of vulgar economicism, however disguised it may be by the addition of stylistic clauses about the dialectical relationship between these two instances. In fact the type of progress of the productive forces is not a neutral and inert factor; on the contrary, it is guided by the relations of production. For instance, the mature tributary mode, as in Egypt and China, proved capable of orienting the progress of the productive forces towards fantastic improvements in irrigation techniques, in building (financed by agricultural progress) and in communications (roads and postal services), thereby reinforcing the tributary mode itself. True, tributary relations of production do limit the development of the productive forces. This was obvious both in China and in the Arab world, where the central authority imposed limits on the corporations. In feudal Europe, the weak link of the tributary societies, the central authority was less powerful — and therefore free towns not yoked to feudalism, and new relations of production, the embryos of capitalism, could appear. These new relations were eventually to allow the bourgeois revolution to accumulate forces and to overthrow all other relations of production, in order to establish new ones capable of carrying the level of development of the productive forces to a higher stage. Elsewhere, within the stronger sectors of tributary society, no similar process was possible and the development of the productive forces could not go beyond a certain level. *Mutatis mutandis*, the same thing is going on today, in terms of the birth of socialist relations of production.

The theses of vulgar Marxism would have us believe that the development of the productive forces is a blind engine which acts everywhere in the same way in its overthrow of previous relations of production. The Asiatic mode of production is of course a source of endless difficulties for those theses. For if the development of productive forces necessarily entails an almost immediate adjustment of the relations of production, where is one to situate this Asiatic mode: Before slavery? Before feudalism? Is it not the case that this viewpoint has, against all the evidence available from a comparison between China and Europe, for example, classified the Asiatic mode as an inferior stage? Surely the implication of this viewpoint is that the societies of the East should have been blocked at a very low level of development of the productive forces. And this, of course, explains the errors of judgement so often made about the Asiatic mode. At best, this total blockage is attributed to geographical conditions! In actual fact, the tributary mode of production, established very early on in its mature form, allowed for a very considerable development of the productive forces (for instance, irrigation in China and Egypt). The stagnation of societies dominated by this mode thus appeared only when the level of development reached was already quite considerable, probably far higher than in any other pre-capitalist society. The thesis which we hold to be truly Marxist, in its rejection of any unique, universal or *a priori* model, is infinitely more convincing. But it situates the social laws at a far more abstract level, the level of modes of production, social formations, the base-superstructure relations particular to a given mode, etc. With these concepts one can account for the different evolution of societies; that is to say one can explain history as it really is, rather than replacing it with a universal but unscientific model.

It is quite true that the laws discovered by historical materialism are universal: the concepts of mode of production or ideology do not apply only to specific societies; the relations which link the social elements to which these concepts refer thus also have a universal importance. But these laws operate in differing contexts. The results to which they lead are thus specific to each case: contradictions always have several possible solutions, albeit on the basis of the same laws. There are thus several evolutionary paths, as opposed to a single road mapped out in advance for the whole of human history. The 'unequal development' thesis emerged primarily from our observations on the various forms in which socialism is making its way in the contemporary world. In the capitalist system, which has reached the imperialist stage characterised by the division of the world into dominant centres and dominated peripheries, the socialist transformation of the world begins by revolutions in the periphery. It begins where the capitalist relations are less developed, where the development of the productive forces therefore makes the transcendence of capitalist relations even more urgent than in the centre, and where, consequently, that transcendence meets with less serious difficulties in the attempt.

On the basis of this first example of unequal development which we are living through today, we went on to ask ourselves whether the same had not been true when pre-capitalist relations were finally displaced by the birth of capitalism. Of course, the lessons of the contemporary world cannot be mechanically applied to the past. Capitalism is the first *world* system and one cannot talk of centre and periphery when one is describing the pre-capitalist systems. We thus came round to the idea that new definitions were called for in the case of the mutually autonomous central and peripheral systems of the pre-capitalist world. We concluded that the most suitable way of using the terms was as follows: the central systems were those which were based on the pre-capitalist mode of production *par excellence*, in its most evolved and mature form, the tributary mode. As for the feudal mode it seemed to us to be a poorer and less finished — let us say, peripheral — form of this tributary mode.

Europe, after the barbarian invasions, was far less advanced than the East or the Mediterranean; it was therefore feudal, just as Japan was feudal compared to tributary China. But this backwardness allowed it to progress faster and more freely. The more evolved Arab world, on the other hand, stagnated. Is this conceptual equipment sufficient to explain the facts, to explain the appearance of capitalism in Europe on the one hand, the abortion of Arab mercantilism on the other? Our answer is: yes. True, if capitalism had not appeared in Europe, humanity would doubtless have discovered it anyhow. But this is not the point. Historical materialism explains history, it accounts for the transformations which have effectively taken place, for failures and successes, that is to say for the manner in which societies have or have not surmounted their contradictions. In other words historical materialism accounts for facts — it does not replace them with a philosophy of history or deal in what would have happened if . . .

Before going into the question of the abortion of Arab mercantilism, we must ask ourselves if it is acceptable to talk about the Arab world in general, whether it can be characterised as a whole. We must remember that we are dealing with an area which stretched over a considerable distance, which is heterogeneous in terms of population and in terms of natural conditions, made up as it is of both impoverished deserts and very fertile and densely populated oases. The history of the millenium which starts with the Muslim conquests and ends with the Arab world's integration into a world system dominated by Europe is hardly more homogeneous, especially as this millenium in some cases has historical roots going back several thousand years. Why should we expect that this slice of human history can be globalised by looking, for instance, for a mode of production characteristic of all its component areas and all its historical periods? Are we wasting our time? Would we not be better occupied in characterising each region in each period, without trying to pick out constants which will quite probably be the mere products of our own bias? Despite the dangers of such generalisations, we are going to take the risk.

Let us first point out that such objections apply to every region of the world: Europe, from the barbarian invasions to the 19th century, is not homogeneous either, nor is the contemporary capitalist world. Nonetheless, one can talk meaningfully about European feudalism, and of the dominant mode of production, in an effort to characterise ten centuries of history North of the Mediterranean. Historical materialism is meaningful only if it enables one to go beyond the specific monograph, if it supplies us with concepts which help us grasp the processes whereby societies — all and any societies — are transformed in their essential respects. The unity of a region or of a period by no means always seems obvious to those who live in it: it is only afterwards that this unity can be seen in the action of the dominant tendencies. Mediaeval Europe has a specific meaning for us today, as it certainly did not for an 11th century knight.

Let us look at the problem from another angle: the contemporary question of Arab unity demands a historical investigation into the roots of that unity, if any. Is Arab unity only the fruit of modern imperialist domination? Is it only a vague cultural aspiration? In our opinion, this unity very definitely does have historical roots. The point is therefore to discover them, to bring out the dominant characteristics specific to that millenium of pre-colonial Arab history. We would not be materialists if we situated these characteristics only in terms of ideology and culture (Islam, the Arabic language) without understanding that these features could not be what they are, were it not that this world has a certain specificity in terms of social formations. We are not talking about mere simplification or denial of differences in time and space. But these differences, which we recognise, are linked to the main specific and dominant tendencies which they both modify and are modified by. This process of abstraction is precisely the scientific contribution of historical materialism. Furthermore, the process by which the pre-colonial Arab world is generally qualified as feudal, by simple analogy with Europe, is a perfect example of false abstraction. It stems from a reduction of universal history to a mechanical model of stages which Marx never stopped protesting against. It neither allows one to understand the reasons for the appearance of capitalism in Europe, nor the tendency towards Arab unity as opposed to the inverse tendency towards national differentiation in Europe.

The articulation of the tributary mode of production with the mercantile relations in the pre-colonial Arab world

In calling the pre-colonial Arab formations mercantile, we have deliberately adopted a provocative terminology. For it is quite obvious that this area of the world, just like all others before the advent of capitalism, was mainly made up of peasants, and exploited peasants at that. Our thesis is as follows: firstly, these agrarian modes of production were either tributary modes (in the wealthier regions) or communal modes (in the poorer and isolated regions), but rarely, if ever, the feudal mode, which appeared only during the decadence of the Arab world; secondly, that mercantile relations were grafted on to these agrarian modes and were articulated with them in a particular way, sometimes dominating the agrarian relations and sometimes dominated by the tributary modes. It is this second aspect of Arab history which gives it its specific characteristics.

The significant facts on which our thesis is founded are the following:

First, the productivity of agriculture South of the Mediterranean was generally much lower than to the North. This is borne out by the practically exclusive use of the classical swing-plough in the Arab world, whilst in Europe the introduction of the deep ploughshare and mould-board soon resulted in decisive qualitative progress. This inferiority of the Arab world was compensated for by the natural fertility of the irrigated areas. This was the case in Egypt, occasionally in Iraq, and also in this or that privileged area at particular times (Andalucia, Cape Bon, the smaller plains of Syria). Nonetheless, the labour productivity of most of the Arab peasantry (excluding Egypt) remained mediocre and stagnant, whilst in Europe an early start in the 11th century led to the flourishing of the so-called agricultural revolution from the 15th to the 18th century, preceding, and paving the way for, the industrial revolution.

Secondly, the productivity of agriculture in the Arab world remained more or less static, in periods of greatness as in periods of decadence. This is very different from what went on in European history. In the Arab world, the periods of prosperity were characterised by an extension of the irrigated zones, to acreage of which fluctuated by factors of 1 to 2 in Egypt and at least 1 to 10 in Iraq. On the whole, fluctuations in population followed those in the extent of the irrigated areas, but techniques hardly changed at all: in Egypt, for instance, from distant antiquity to the 19th century, agricultural technique was always based on flood-irrigation and the swing-plough. In Europe the growth in population was continuous, slow at times and accelerating at others, in proportion to the progress of agricultural productivity; in the Arab world the fluctuations in population were sudden and violent.

Thirdly, the Arab world's periods of greatness coincided with the periods of flourishing trade. Of course, the great strides made by commerce did not benefit the Arab world as a whole. In the Mashreq the trade routes passed through Syria which, with Iraq, was the main beneficiary (indeed this is the period when the centre of the Caliphate was situated in the area: first in Damascus, then in Baghada). When the Turco-Mongol invasions ravaged the area, the trade routes shifted towards the South and the Red Sea, to the great benefit of Egypt under the Ayubids and Mameluks of the 12th and 14th centuries. In the Maghreb, the trade routes shifted from West to East, from the Moroccan Tafilalt to Tunis and Libyan Tripoli, and there was a corresponding shift in the main centres of prosperity, both in the Maghreb and in the sub-Saharan Sahel. However this does not yet tell us which was cause and which was consequence: was the autonomous progress of agriculture the basis which made the commercial developments possible or was it the growth of trade which induced agricultural progress in its wake? Our interpretation of the facts inclines us to choose the second hypothesis, precisely because the agricultural progress was more extensive (expansion of irrigated acreage and of population) than intensive (increases in productivity).

Fourthly, what was the relative importance of the surpluses drawn by the ruling classes from the exploitation of the peasantry and from the profits of commerce (and of manufacture of artisan production)? Again, we must clarify what we understand of the meaning and nature of recorded facts. The specialists have not yet finished their inventories of Arab finances at different periods of this long history and for each of its regions. The fact that, on the whole, the revenue drawn from ground rent (including taxes) was quantitatively predominant proves nothing: until the advent of capitalism every human society was predominantly agrarian and, from the first village chiefdoms to the greatest empires, the main source of funds for the ruling class remained the exploitation of peasants. But one must go beyond this rather obvious point. One must enquire whether the rent extracted from the peasants was merely enough to feed the ruling class and its direct servants, or whether this rent was adequate enough to allow for secondary circuits of manufacture (artisans, workshops, etc.). to be grafted on to it. It is not enough to ascertain the relative importance of these secondary circuits (measured, for example, in terms of a proportion of the urbanised population); one must know whether, in their turn, these secondary circuits made it possible — by means of commercial exchange — to draw on surplus generated by foreign agriculture. One must find out how mercantile relations were articulated with agrarian relations, whether the flourishing of the former was merely the consequence of progress in agriculture, or whether, on the contrary, the progress in agriculture was induced by a growth in commercial prosperity, in which case the mercantile relations would have exercised a domination over the whole of the system. Direct statistics tell us little at this level, for what is needed is an in-depth analysis of prices, formation of revenues, the causal mechanisms determining the system, etc. The problem is analogous to that posed by the theory of 'unequal exchange' in contemporary society. Our thesis is that the same approach is relevant to Arab history: one can only understand the towns in their periods of greatness by reintegrating the Arab world into a larger whole, within which the surplus circulated and became concentrated in a particular way.

Our thesis, however, does not imply that the appearance of the state in this area of the world was the outcome of commerce. Here, as elsewhere, the state's appearance was bound up with the internal formation of classes and with the exploitation stemming from the latter. And here, as elsewhere, material production was largely agricultural at this stage of development of the productive forces. The exploitation on which the appearance of the state was founded could thus only be that of the peasant producers, in one way or another. But there are states and states: a district chiefdom is hardly the same thing as an empire covering thousands of miles, including millions of inhabitants, containing prosperous towns in which a numerous population is concentrated.

Once we have grasped the origin of the state in the area, and the modalities of the internal exploitation of the peasants on which it was based, we are only just beginning to broach the question, for the surplus generated by the majority of peasants in the area remained small (except in Egypt, and, occasionally, in Iraq). The fact remains that in some periods enormous towns, which were amongst the most prosperous in history, developed, whilst in other periods, the same areas were brought low by decadence without there being any significant change in agricultural production. Generally speaking, the peaks of civilisation in the Maghreb and the Mashreq were characterised by a very pronounced urbanisation which absorbed up to a third or even a half of the population of the area, which is quite exceptional historically. On the other hand, Egypt retained a predominantly rural economy which was more stable. Not that there were no towns in Egypt: on the contrary, there were a great many small and medium sized towns, with very solid links to rural regional territories with which there was considerable and stable exchange; there were also some large ones — Alexandria and Cairo — but these were capital cities grafted on to empires which stretched beyond the confines of Egypt. We have taken all these nuances into account.

What our thesis suggests is simply that one cannot truly appreciate the nature of a social system in all its complexity, if one isolates that system from the larger whole into which it is integrated. As far as the Arab world is concerned, one cannot ignore the role played by the various regions which make it up, in the overall Europe/Mediterranean/Western and Southern Asia/Sudan system. Of course one must enquire into the generation of the surplus in each part of the whole. But one must also ask how that surplus circulated and how it eventually came to be concentrated in certain places at certain times within the area as a whole. To avoid this problem is to avoid an essential aspect of reality. And this is where the problematic of long distance trade comes in.

Who today would dare explain the wealth of the Gulf Emirates only in terms of the exploitation of nomads and oil industry workers, without taking into consideration the world capitalist system into which those states are integrated? Who would venture to deny that the prosperity of Great Britain was linked to the exploitation of its empire and that the decline of the latter has played its part in the decline of the old metropolis? Who would dare to account for the wealth of the Netherlands by concentrating exclusively on the exploitation of its peasantry, without taking into account the role of the mercantilist trade the Dutch once controlled? To ignore the problematic of the circulation of the surplus is effectively to reduce historical materialism to a simple dogma according to which reality is contained in each morsel of the totality; a dogma which would make it acceptable to study each society in isolation. This dogmatism has always exercised a certain attraction: it ties in with the keen typologist's love of classification and with the idealist attempt to force reality into simple pre-determined schemata. If we wanted quotes to prove that this is no part of the Marxist method, we could easily find hundreds of pages in which Marx talks of trade in terms reaching far beyond the elementary mechanisms of exploitation.

One cannot understand anything about the Arab world if one does not grasp these issues as a whole. Especially at the level of ideology, it is important to assess whether the surplus was drawn from the local exploitation of the peasantry or from the exploitation of trade by which a surplus generated elsewhere was transferred to the Arab world. Who would venture to reduce all the pre-capitalist societies to a single, supposedly feudal model, to ignore the specificities of their ideologies and to ask no questions about the nature, origin and consequences of these specificities? When we speak of trading formations, as opposed to peasant formations, we are seeking to accentuate three specificities, both in terms of their economic base (the circulation and centralisation of the surplus within a system considered as a whole) and in terms of their ideology.

But why not accept a definition of the special merchant character of the Arab world in terms of its civilisation, making a distinction between an area's civilisation and its nature as a social formation? Because this distinction is sterile. It stems from a reduction of the concept of formation to an economic level, which involves lumping together all the other features of that society, its ideologies, politics, religions, cultures, original traits, etc., in a catch-all concept of civilisation, superimposed on the economic. For us, historical materialism must account simultaneously for the whole of a society's characteristics, including those which are traditionally confined within the ambit of the study of civilisations. As it happens, the merchant character of the Arab world has deep roots in the social formation. By integrating the trade relations into the formation, one comes to understand not only the mode of surplus circulation but also the particularities of the superstructure: the merchant ideology. Our method allows us to deal with both the issue of Arab unity and the divergent paths in the respective evolutions of European and Arab history.

What then was the essential nature of the Arab formations, feudal or otherwise? And how was the merchant character of this formation articulated with its agrarian base? What are the specificities, what are the dominant features and at what level are they situated: at the base, in the superstructure, or both?

The root of the problem lies in the pseudo-Marxist bad habit of confusing (pre-capitalist) landowners and feudalists, a simplification which has little to do with Marx.

The feudal mode of production belongs to a vast family of tributary modes of production, all characterised by the division of the population into working peasants (in some cases organised in village communities, in others not) and landowning masters, and correspondingly characterised by the division of the social product into peasant means of subsistence and tribute (generally in kind) drawn by the ruling class. From this first very abstract approach, we can now move closer to the concrete, as Marx did in his analysis of the capitalist mode.

The tributary modes of production were sometimes articulated with long distance trade, notably in cases where the tribute was sufficient also to feed other producers (artisans), a part of whose product could then be exported, thereby enabling the importation of luxury goods for the ruling classes. In such cases the trade was carried out by merchants, not by capitalist businessmen. Such was the case of feudal Europe. But long distance trade does not itself necessarily involve tribute in this way. For the merchants can be intermediaries between tributary societies which have practically no direct contact with each other, and these merchants can live off the profits they draw from their role as intermediaries. Such was largely the case of the Arab merchants. In formations of the first type the tributary (feudal) mode of production is dominant, whilst the simple petty-merchant mode (artisans) is articulated with long distance trade on the basis of this dominant mode. In formations of the second type, the tributary mode of production was generally not dominant; it became so only in the brief moments when the general prosperity led to the enhancement of irrigatable land, as happened during the three centuries of Abassid greatness in Iraq and Syria. It ceased to be dominant whenever agriculture fell back on isolated peasant areas, during the long centuries of decadence.

It was thus only during the periods of Arab greatness —which are also the periods of Arab unity — that the tributary (not the feudal) mode of production became dominant. Even then, and precisely because in this case the surplus drawn from the peasantry was small, the tributary mode of production remained limited in its geographical extent as in its intensity, to Egypt and Iraq. Entire regions of the Arab world remained the realm of free peasantries organised into communities. In other areas the tribute remained light, at least in absolute terms. This is the reason for the constant precariousness of Arab feudalism, and for its dependence on the central authority (hence the frequent links between the fief and state service, and the general absence of the hereditary principle). The central authority therefore based its wealth and its power less on tribute drawn from the peasants than on profits from long distance trade. When this trade began to disappear, Arab society regressed and the distinguishing characteristics of feudalism emerged: a falling-back on to impoverished countrysides (except in Egypt), the emergence of the hereditary principle as applied in feudal relations, and the corresponding weakening of central authority. At the time of the colonial conquests, the Arab world presented just such a picture of impoverished feudalism.

Let us recapitulate. The preponderant mode of production in Arab agriculture is the tributary mode, not the feudal mode which only appears in periods of decadence. The merchant relations had a dominant effect on these formations, and this manifested itself in the fact that these relations were the motor of prosperity which promoted tributary agricultural development when times were good, but were grafted on to feudalism when times were bad. The particularities of Egypt, which was always more stable than the rest of the Arab world, were not capable of negating those features which characterised Arab history globally and determined its course. We have here a first explanation for the abortiveness of the Arab formation's evolution towards capitalism.

The question of Arab mercantilism's failure

The question of Arab trade's failure to evolve towards capitalism presents no real problem; bourgeois historiography has created a false issue. This historiography begins by confusing money and capital, commerce and capitalism; it then discovers evidence of capitalism everywhere, in Ancient China, in the Greek and Roman world, or amongst the Arabs, and asks itself why only European capitalism succeeded. Religion (Protestantism, in Weber's view) or race (Germanic superiority or, more subtly, the inheritance of the Greeks) turn out to be the only way out of this blind alley.

Money and trade, in fact appeared well before capitalism. They appeared as soon as producers disposed of sufficient surplus and when the division of labour allowed for the exchange of products in which this available surplus could be incorporated. Indeed the bulk of the exchanges in pre-capitalist society, notably the exchanges between small producers within the same society (peasants and artisans in the same village) took place without any intermediaries, or indeed money, coming into it at all. However, as soon as a significant fraction of the surplus was centralised in the hands of powerful privileged classes (feudalists, royal courts, etc.) that fraction could be used in long distance trade, that is in the exchange of products, especially luxury products, between different societies. A merchant intermediary could then draw profit from his monopoly position in this contact. The laws of profit relating to commercial capital thus do not apply to this intermediary profit, which is rooted in the difference in subjective values (different ways of appreciating social utilities) of two societies which were relatively unaware of each other. For, here again, Marx insists on the role of commercial capital in the equalisation of the rate of profit in the capitalist mode of production. The profits of capitalist commercial capital come from the redistribution of surplus value (a form of surplus specific to capitalism) generated within society; a transformation of surplus value in its form as profit. The profits of pre-capitalist commercial trade stemmed from the transfer of surplus between one society and another. The function of this long distance trade was fulfilled by specialised strata, often by classes or ethnic groups ('people-classes'), such as the Jews in Mediaeval Europe, or by societies which had developed mainly on this basis, such as Phoenicia, Greece, the Hanse, the Italian cities and the Arab world at its height.

The concentration of monetary wealth in the hands of these merchant social groups was not capitalism and could not naturally lead to capitalism. The appearance of capitalism requires a disintegration of the pre-capitalist mode of production, which engenders a proletarianisation, a separation of the producers from their means of production, thereby paving the way for a free labour market.

Why did the concentration of monetary wealth in the Arab world not lead to the disintegration of the pre-capitalist modes of production in the countryside, and thus lead to capitalism? Apparently favourable circumstances were characteristic of that world, as is clearly reflected in Muslim law. The monetary form of ground rent had become standard centuries before. The Arabs also had free labour, and wage-labour was frequent in the towns and even in certain rural areas. One could even talk about a proletariat and a lumpen proletariat, without fear of anachronism. Surely all this should have led to capitalism?

Two theses have been advanced to account for the Arab world's blocked evolution; each contains a part of the truth. The first of these theses states that at the very moment when favourable conditions had accumulated to the point of preparing for a qualitative change — an industrial revolution — there was a brutal modification of the trade circuits which put an end to the ongoing process. This modification must naturally be attributed to the Turco-Mongol invasions. But this thesis — which is very popular in the Arab world — is debatable. Whatever the extent of destruction, especially in Iraq and Syria, the trade circuits should surely have been re-established under Ottoman rule when peace had returned. In fact, the trade circuits shifted southwards, to the advantage of 13th and 14th century Egypt. True, the constant threat from outside contributed to the militarisation of the Arab world. But was the militarisation an obstacle to the prosperity of trade? The alliance of warriors and merchants has been noted elsewhere; why not here? Whatever the explanation, the fact remains that the change resulted in a sudden drying-up of the accumulation of money and the collapse of the merchant world, which entered into a long period of decadence. Did not the same misfortunes ruin the Italian cities? In the end, it was North-west (Atlantic) Europe, England and France, which were the ultimate inheritors from this long process of maturation and which ruined the hopes of both of their ancient Arab and Italian precursors, and even of their immediate predecessors, the Spanish and the Portuguese.

The second thesis lays more stress on the exceptionally favourable characteristics of the European world's internal relations, as opposed to the internal relations in other parts of the world, even strongly mercantilised ones such as, amongst others, the Arab world and China. Only Europe (and Japan) had a truly feudal mode of production. The point is that this feudal mode of production is particularly liable to disintegration under the pressure of the development of merchant relations, since in the feudal mode power is not centralised but scattered amongst the various feudal masters of the land. Under these conditions, the mercantilisation of the product and of rent leads to the rural populations' rapid exclusion from access to the relative surplus; in other words to a massive and rapid proletarianisation, as happened most strikingly in England, where the majority of the population was proletarianised between 1750 and 1815. In the Arab world, on the contrary, the majority of the peasantry remained outside the system or on its edges, in areas whose isolation was reinforced by poverty. Except in Egypt; but even in Egypt the central authority remained, as it did in China, infinitely more powerful than its equivalent in feudal Europe. And this powerful authority, which is characteristic of the tributary mode in its mature form, kept the peasants on the land by means of an agrarian policy specifically geared to that end. Indeed this opposition, between the feudal mode — which we can call peripheral — and the tributary mode in its developed form, has been attributed to the barbarian origins of feudalism, the roots of which lie in the Germanic communitarian modes: this opposition is most probably the first major manifestation of the law of 'unequal development'.

Still thanks to these specific characteristics of the feudal mode, Europe (and Japan) were to benefit from exceptional conditions on the level of the organisation of political power. In Europe the kings, in order to counterbalance the power of the feudalists, were forced to support the merchant world; the latter had in fact already managed to establish itself firmly in free towns not subject to feudal authority which was almost purely rural. Nothing similar happened elsewhere. In the Arab world the greater power of the central authority (if not at the level of the whole Arab empire, then certainly at the level of each of the countries which made it up) precluded the growth of free towns. There were, of course, craft corporations, associations of merchants and artisans. These groups had even been known to have some share in the government of the Arab towns. But there were no free towns which escaped totally from feudal power and feudal law, as happened in feudal Europe. The Arab corporations were never the masters of the cities.

All the historians insist on the close surveillance which was kept on these corporations, both in the Arab world and in China. For the social force which threatened the central authority was not that of the feudalists — who did not exist, since the landowning aristocracy was an urban aristocracy of functionaries — but that of the merchants. And when the central authority in the Arab world weakened to the point of being incapable of operating in some areas, decadence had already set in: commerce was ruined and the peasantries quickly took the opportunity to assert their local autonomy.

What really needs explaining is thus not so much the Arab (or Chinese) failure, but Europe's (or Japan's) success, a success which stems from the peripheral character of the feudal mode. The failure of Arab mercantilism is no mystery. Of course, had Europe not become capitalist as quickly as it did, then doubtless the operating contradictions within other societies (Arab, Chinese, Indian, etc.) would have been resolved by the emergence of capitalist relations based in those societies. But this is a side issue.

The thesis which we accept situates the nature of social laws on the level we have described, and thus allows one to understand how the precocious appearance of capitalism in Europe was related to the singularities of feudalism. The distinguishing features which separate the development of a European world economy, as it emerged from the 16th century onwards, on the one hand, from the expansion of earlier tributary empires, on the other, highlight the singularity of the transition to capitalism and thereby force us to reflect on fundamental issues of historical materialism. The geographical expansion of other societies had never taken this form. The centralised tributary Chinese state integrated newly colonised Southern regions as ordinary provinces, which were brought under a single system of extraction of centralised surplus, drawn off by a bureaucracy of prebendaries. European expansion, on the contrary, created the first real periphery on the basis of an unequal specialisation of labour. The empire was a political unit, whilst the European world system is an economic system; in other words the links which join the different parts of the latter are economic links, not necessarily or mainly political links. This is no fortuitous coincidence: rather it reveals essential aspects of the way the relations between the base and the superstructure operate in different modes of production.

These conceptual clarifications enable us to gain a better understanding of the nature of European feudal society, of the reasons behind the particular forms taken by its expansion, and of the original genesis of capital. If feudal Europe was not an empire, it is because the feudal mode is a peripheral and unfinished form of the tributary mode. The origins of the (feudal) dismemberment of state power and non-centralisation of surplus can be traced back to the way in which the Roman Empire was overtaken by barbarians who had only just progressed beyond the communal mode. The primitive forms of the tributary mode are thus more flexible than the finished forms: it was backward Europe, not the advanced East, which developed the capitalist transcendence of the tributary mode. This manifestation of unequal development gives the lie to the thesis of a continual linear development of the productive forces which would supposedly determine the successive modes of production.

Thus pre-capitalist trade could only bring about the rapid formation of the capitalist mode where it was grafted on a peripheral mode, namely feudalism. Had it been grafted on to the tributary mode, it could easily have aborted; in that case, in the absence of a rapid appearance of capitalism in Europe and its subsequent extension to a dominated Arab world, the course of history would doubtless have been both longer and very different.

ZIONISM, ISRAEL AND THE FUTURE OF PALESTINE

If Israel were a state like any other, a compromise would always be possible in the area, a compromise which would express the existing relation of forces. But Israel is based on a very special type of ideology. It is because of this ideology that the downturn in Jewish immigration at the beginning of the Sixties was seen as a crisis; without that immigration, Zionism falls apart and Israel becomes an ordinary state, the state of its inhabitants, who can then coexist with other peoples and other states. Zionism needs wars and annexations in order to maintain its links with the Jews of the Diaspora. This ideological basis may even make all negotiations pointless.

If the fate of Arab nationalism and of the Arab nation today seems to depend on the actions of Zionism, it is only proof that nationalism is still impotent. It does not mean that it must stay impotent, since a socialist revolution in the Arab world would give this nationalism the power to reduce the problem of Israel to its proper dimensions. Such a power would force Israel to abandon Zionism and to become an ordinary state. Negotiations would then be meaningful, because it would be based on political, not ideological grounds. El Fatah's programme for a Palestinian state, which is a political programme, sketches a possible solution. It must take all the bad faith of the West not to see the gulf which separates the Fatah's political approach to a solution from Zionism's ideological and mystical rejection of any solution short of genocide against Arabs or the submission of a rightless Arab minority (or majority). It is only in South Africa, a state also animated by a racist ideology, apartheid, that such barriers to change are erected.

Zionism can only survive if it succeeds in becoming the dominant sub-imperialism in the area. If this fails, must Israel disappear and its population return to wander the Diaspora? There is another possible solution: the levantisation of a small oriental Jewish state integrated into the region. At the moment it is this levantisation which the Zionists fear above all else. For the population of Palestine is already mostly oriental: more than half of the inhabitants in Israel and the occupied territories are Arabs; more than half of the Jews themselves are Orientals. Zionism never succeeded in drawing a significant proportion of the Western Jews, who are nearly all Ashkenasi, to Palestine. On the other hand, the vast majority of the Sepharadim, mostly Arab Jews, left the Maghreb and the Middle East to emigrate to Israel. The chauvinistic policy of Arab reaction was just what Zionism needed. These Oriental Jews are at home in Jerusalem, in Fez or Baghdad, just as non-Jewish Arabs are at home from the Atlantic to the Gulf. They could thus become a specific community established in part of Palestine.

Zionism has no choice but to perpetuate the racist domination exercised by the European minority over both the Oriental Jews and the non-Jewish Arabs. The success of such a policy is largely due to the fact that the Arabs did not manage to offer the Oriental Jews another option. If an Arab Palestinian state were to coexist tomorrow with a Jewish state, and given that the expansionist Zionist perspective was excluded, dramatic changes would take place. Powerful forces would push towards a levantisation of the Jewish state: European Jews would either leave, as the *Pieds Noirs* left Algeria, because they could not envisage treating as equals those they considered their inferiors, or they would accept their own orientalisation.

This possibility should not be excluded. After all, it amounts to seeing this part of the Middle East as it always has been: a federation of cantons. Neither Christian, Druse and Moslem Lebanon, nor Jewish and Muslim Palestine, nor the Syria of the interior and Alid Syria, have ever been integrated into a single homogenous nation, such as Egypt for instance. But diversity, which today presupposes mutual respect and considerable autonomy, does not preclude economic, political and even cultural unity.

6

THE PERSPECTIVES FACING THE ARAB WORLD: SOME POSSIBLE OUTCOMES

Will it be a reunited, modernised, rich and powerful Arab world which emerges from the testing times history has imposed on it during the last few centuries and especially during the last fifty years? Or will it be an Arab world bogged down in an impoverishing traditionalism, thereby prolonging its division and its impotence?

We neither seek to answer this question crudely, nor to go into the complex issues involved in an abstract theoretical debate about the still ambiguous meanings of such terms as modernity and tradition, capitalism and socialism, wealth and poverty. We will only attempt to give the beginnings of an answer by envisaging several possible outcomes, distinguishable because based on possible combinations of these elements.

A FIRST POSSIBILITY: A NEO-COLONIAL ORDER AND ARAB DISUNITY

The first possibility is the one defined by the prolongation of the tendencies which have dominated the area during the last twenty years. The Arab world would then remain divided into independent states. In the oil producing countries the process of extroverted and dependent development would accelerate. Some countries, such as Algeria and Iraq, would attempt to carry out an integrated industrialisation based on simultaneously setting up capital goods industries and consumption industries. This industrialisation would adopt advanced capitalist technologies: it would therefore soon run into the problem of the necessity for foreign outlets if expansion was to continue. Others, the desert countries which cannot absorb their oil revenue, would tend to invest abroad in order to draw dividends from investment. They would soon run into the nationalism of the developed countries, as resistance to increasing Arab takeovers grew. Thanks to the disunity of the Arab world, no solution would be found to the Palestinian problem: Jordan could be held at arm's length indefinitely, whilst the prosperity of Lebanon would continue to be based on the concentration of services in its capital city, given that the old order could be re-established in that country, which remains highly dubious. Southern Arabia, Sudan, Morocco, Tunisia, Syria and Egypt are the misfits in this possible outcome. But this state of affairs could not last for long and would make the continuation of the old model of economic growth in the Arab world extremely unlikely. For Egypt remains the key: its fragility necessarily implies that of the area as a whole. Let us add that this possible programme of development is based on the continuing expansion of the developed centres along the lines which have emerged during the last twenty years. That expansion, however, is now entering a crisis which we believe to be structural, deep-seated and lasting.[1]

A FAMILY OF NEW POSSIBILITIES: THE ARAB WORLD AS A RELAY IN A RENOVATED IMPERIALIST ORDER

We must thus put the possible outcomes in the context of the global crisis of the world capitalist system; in the context of a revision of the terms of the international division of labour; in the context of the setting up of a new international economic order which will be accompanied by changes in the equilibrium of forces, both on a world scale (equilibrium between world powers, international alliances, etc.) and on a local scale (class alliances). In this framework one can already see the broad outlines of the outcome appearing in the form of an Arab renaissance, an affirmation of Arab power.

The second possibility could be defined as follows. The resources of Western technology, the financial weight of Arab oil wealth, and the abundant, proletarianised, skilled cheap labour of several countries, notably Egypt, would be pooled. The result would be to integrate a gradually unifying Arab world into a new international division of labour — as a partner of imperialism. This local development within the overall logic of the world capitalist system[2] would give the Arab bourgeoisie a new lease on life. Industrialisation could proceed beyond the import-substitution stage: the simpler bottlenecks which hold up integrated development in small countries would be overcome.

Are we talking about a stage in a road which would lead to the Arab world turning into a new Japan, that is to say an independent, developed and powerful part of the capitalist world? Can one talk in this context t radical modernisation? We believe, on the contrary, that Japan was the last country ever to achieve full development by the capitalist road, because it was the last ever to launch its development before the formation of imperialism. Imperialism, by extension of its means of control throughout the planet, by its domination and exploitation of the countries of Asia, Africa and Latin America in order to feed the profits of the monopolies at the centre, has already made any attempt at autonomous capitalist development in the periphery of the system irrelevant. There are no known historical experiences of a productive economy being constituted as a result of a gradually internalised input from abroad and the maintenance of wide openings on to the outside world.[3] This is why the unequal development of the periphery by no means implies that certain underdeveloped countries are gradually drawing closer to the economic take-off point, as Rostow suggests. Rather it implies that countries will be adapted to increasingly differentiated roles within the hierarchised world imperialist system, in the framework of an unequal division of labour, reserving the function of imperialist relay for some countries and that of neo-colonial reserves for others.[4] This type of dependent development has very narrow possibilities, since the domination of the centres, its modalities having been renewed, would perpetuate itself by the monopoly of technology and the gradual penetration of Western patterns of consumption. Also, whilst the local bourgeoisie would probably draw a certain advantage from this type of development, which might even allow it in certain cases to widen its support base by extending the layers of the petty bourgeoisie, this would not be an answer. The popular masses, who are necessarily excluded from the advantages of this type of prosperity, would be condemned to pauperisation and permanent unemployment. This sort of development, which destroys national societies by ruining their culture, is nothing but a lumpen development; this modernisation nothing but a lumpen-Europeanisation. This is all that the Brazilian model amounts to, in Iran, in Egypt, in Algeria. In this sense, modernisation is in no way synonymous with progress, with liberation, with independence — not to speak of socialism.

This model of modernisation is nonetheless the one chosen by the Arab bourgeoisies. In order to cope with immediate difficulties, they have opted for a sub-let industrialisation aimed at exporting to the developed centres and to the neo-colonial reserve areas. In other words they have chosen to sell the national labour power to foreign monopolies cheaply. The super-profits drawn from this super-exploitation are, for the most part, exported either by visible mechanisms (transferred profits, foreign debts, cost of imported technology, etc.) or by invisible ones inherent in the price structure. The local bourgeoisie also draws its marginal share of these super-profits. Within this framework, the Arab bourgeoisie is already willing to associate itself with Israel, which would supply the technology. Furthermore, American imperialism is now prepared to join in this particular game, and to modify its alliances appropriately. There are several variants on this possible outcome. Each is a function of possible foreign alliances, possible arrangements made with respect to local leadership, possible class alliances within the Arab world.

The strongest way of establishing this outcome would be based on Saudi leadership of a grand alliance of state bourgeoisies, kulak bourgeoisies and reconciled compradors which would handle the affairs of Egypt and the other states.

Another possible modality, though hardly the most likely today, would be characterised by the predominance of the state capitalist style at home and of the Soviet alliance in foreign affairs.

Generally speaking, can one freely combine these three characteristics: Arab unity or Arab dismemberment, internal dominance of state capital or of private capital, an American or a Soviet foreign alliance? To sort out this web of interlinked problems we must first dwell on the preliminary basic issues which are twofold: the class nature of Soviet society and the aims of the Soviet state's strategy; the orientation of American (and European) imperialism.

Preliminary issues

The unequal development of the Arab world requires us to distinguish between two easily confused sets of struggles. The first kind of struggle is the one waged in countries in which the old forms of imperialist domination, based on the alliance with the latifundist-comprador bourgeoisie, are still entrenched. Here the struggle is between these conservative forces and those of a potential state capitalism, the forces of socialism being sometimes still mixed in with the latter. The second kind of struggle is that waged in the other countries where state capitalism has already been established and where a radical return to the past seems unlikely. Here the struggle is between the conservative forces which seek to halt evolution and those which seek to push it forwards.

The drift to the right should therefore not be interpreted as the final defeat of petty bourgeois nationalism (and of Soviet influence, to which it is linked) by the forces of the old pro-Western formations. There is no point in entertaining illusions: state capitalism corresponds to very deep-seated tendencies, its roots are firmly planted both within the internal social evolution of the Arab world and in the international balance of forces with its system of Third World domination. For years, unwarranted stress has been placed on the contradiction between state capitalism and liberal capitalism. (Socialism often having been confused with dependent state capitalism). But the events of the last few years confirm that this contradiction is secondary. The agrarian reforms and the nationalisations can only be reversed with great difficulty; they have already created firmly based social structures. A true restoration of the old social order is thus well nigh impossible.

More plausibly, there could actually be a fusion between the new forms of state capitalism and the old forms of private capital. This has already been attempted in the state capitalist countries, by the absorption of the old comprador and latifundist bourgeoisie into the state capitalist system, a fusion of the old bourgeoisie with the new rural kulak bourgeoisie and with the state bourgeoisie. The Nasserist experience is a good example of this, at least until 1963. As proof that such a fusion is a response to objective tendencies, one only has to look at the progress made by state capitalism in the 'liberal' countries such as Morocco or the Gulf States.

If tendencies of this sort are so strong it is fundamentally because the state bourgeoisie's vision of modernisation and participation in the world system is not essentially in contradiction with that of the kulak or even comprador bourgeoisies. What makes such a fusion difficult is partly the contradictions between the two sections of the bourgeoisie, state bourgeoisie and private bourgeoisie, and partly the contradiction which opposes the masses and the bourgeoisie as a whole, however confusedly.

The first kind of contradiction is aggravated by the major contradiction which opposes the people and the bourgeoisie; the game is therefore rigged in favour of state capitalism to the extent that the latter can appear as a transition towards socialism. The contradictions are also amplified by the superimposition of foreign alliances, by the fact that the U.S.S.R. supports one side of the bourgeoisie and the U.S. supports another. Finally these contradictions are compounded by Arab disunity and the competition for leadership of the Arab world as a whole.

State capitalism is not a transition towards socialism. This is why we have been so harsh in our judgement of Nasserism; not that this means that we justify the retrograde steps which followed it, of course. Nasser's goal (whatever the ideological false consciousness disguising its nature) at least until 1963, was to harness Arab unity in order to use the financial resources drawn from oil as a means towards a more advanced industrialisation and integration into the world system. The Soviet alliance was essential to the Egyptian state bourgeoisie, which had appeared earlier than elsewhere, and in international conditions very different from those of today. From 1963 onwards, of course, as the major contradictions between the masses and the authorities made itself felt in Egypt, state capitalism moved leftwards; was this demagogic pre-emption the result of an evolution in the balance of forces or even in Nasser's personal evolution (he moved closer to the revisionist communists towards the end of his life)? Whatever the case may be, the fact remains that the system failed to develop a stable equilibrium.

How then did the Soviet intervention graft itself on to these internal class struggles?

Neither the U.S. nor the U.S.S.R. can give up the idea of dominating the area. Having been kicked out of Eastern Asia by the victory of the Vietnamese, Laotian and Cambodian people, the imperialists have fallen back on the Indian Ocean, where a chain of major bases has been hastily set up by Iran (Abu Musa and the Gulf coast), by Britain (Oman) and by the U.S. (Bahrain and especially Diego Garcia). These bases, complementing those in the Eastern Mediterranean (Cyprus, Turkey and Greece), surround the Middle East. Americans and Russians are now fighting for political control over the West coast of the Indian Ocean in Yemen, in Somalia, in Tanzania, in Mozambique and in Madagascar.

Above all, one must examine the nature of Soviet state power. Firstly, because the foreign policy of a country is always a reflection of the nature of its state power. Secondly, because there is an existing Arab communism which follows Moscow and has developed a method of seeing things and analysing problems which one has to take into account. Finally, because the Arab peoples, whose historic enemy is Western imperialism, have until recently gone through the experience of an alliance with the Soviet Union against this enemy.

Our thesis is that Soviet Society has gradually become a new class society. The USSR's official foreign policy is therefore a quite ordinary phenomenon which has to be taken into account. This new class society is on the rise with respect to capitalist society — which is declining — because the new class society is better suited to the development of the productive forces, which requires an increasing centralisation of capital. Hence the possibility of a new type of imperialism developing in the future, social imperialism, which may gain ground as it forces out the classical forms of imperialism. But even more importantly, the Soviet model, because it suits the deep-rooted spontaneous movement of the productive forces, may continue to enjoy popular support and therefore preserve the ideological confusion of revisionism. This is why revisionist communism sees state capitalism as a real transition, if not as socialism itself. But this policy forces the USSR to rely mainly on the state bourgeoisies. Soviet strategy thereby ties in with the internal tendencies of the development of state capitalism in the Arab world.

All this implies a natural alliance between the USSR and Arab state capitalism, in opposition to the natural alliance between the United States and Arab private capital. This is not mainly a question of ideological sympathy; rather it is a matter of popular pressures mystified by revisionist analysis. Above all, it is because the Soviet Union has offered the Arab bourgeoisies, disguised as the state, the possibility of an infinitely more rapid industrial development. Imperialism could not match the Soviet Union's generous offer, and till today, despite the possible beginnings of a change in Western strategy, it is not clear that the West will be as willing as the Russians to help the industrialisation of the Arab world. One could even say that if the West has initiated this change it is in order to compete with the Soviet Union: and if the Arab bourgeoisies are today perhaps capable of forcing imperialism to make concessions, it is because they have been reinforced by the Russian alliance.

The fact remains that although these alliances are still in force, tactical upheavals are always a possibility. On the Arab side, the state bourgeoisie, because it is the bourgeoisie of dependent countries shaped by the imperialist system, has never ceased to look to the West. Every section of this bourgeoisie, which admires the American pattern of consumption and has been alienated by a hundred years of Western domination, essentially prefers the West. For the USSR can only offer it a poorer model of the West. On the Russian side, the USSR, in the pursuit of its world aims, can, for this or that reason resulting from negotiation-confrontation with the United States, suddenly change its tactics in the Middle East. Indeed

Soviet diplomacy has already been seen to put pressure on 'left-wing' Syria when the latter sought to assist the Palestinians in Jordan; the USSR thereby paved the way for the shift to the right in Damascus.

How probable are the various modalities of a new dependence?

The first modality — tripartite American, Saudi and Sadatist leadership — remains difficult to put into practice, despite its apparent successes: the Palestinian problem and the current orientation of Algeria and Iraq weaken its chances. But the main difficulty comes from Egypt itself: the open class struggle, which constantly grows more intense and dominates Egyptian life, ruins the stabilisation projects. Arab and Western capital is still worried and dares not venture into this hornet's nest.

Furthermore, it should never be forgotten that Western imperialism is still fundamentally suspicious of Egypt. This is an old tradition: even in the days of Mohamed Ali, Europe took pains to abort a modernisation which might have turned Egypt into a precocious version of Japan. Today, American imperialism still fears that a strong and industrialised Egypt — even a reactionary one — could undertake on its own account an Arab reunification, thereby threatening U.S. interests in the Gulf area.

Let us add that this first modality would derive its strength from the reconciliation of state and private bourgeoisies, a possibility which is far from being welcomed in the United States, both on the internal and international level.

The problem is that there are no significant revolutionary forces to propose another possibility to the masses. After the class restoration carried out by Sadat, the opposition made a point of contrasting the new regime with Nasserism. The communists themselves, still deeply entrenched in the fundamental theses of revisionism, which confuse socialism and state capitalism, did not dare set themselves apart from the Nasserist current once and for all. Even amongst the Palestinians, the break with these theses is still far from having been made. The Arab Nationalist Movement (Harakat al Qawmiyin), from which the most radical wing of Arab communism has emerged to spread throughout the East and inspire the revolutions in South Yemen and Dhofar, makes up the only embryo of a Maoist critique of revisionism. But it does not yet dominate the Egyptian scene, which remains the key to Arab problems. This is why a radical critique of Nasserism is essential, and must be carried out in association with a critique of revisionism, by which we mean not only the critique of Soviet state policy but also, and especially, a critique of this pseudo-Marxism, of its theoretical basis and of its strategy.

Under such conditions, the modalities of this possible 'imperialist relay' outcome continue to depend mainly on external factors and on secondary and contingent internal factors such as the ever possible coup d'etats, from the left or from the right.

This is why we do not want to exclude the second modality of this possibility, characterised by the predominance of state capitalism at home, and of the Soviet alliance in foreign affairs.

This modality will remain seriously on the cards if the crisis of the capitalist system deepens and leads to collapse in Europe or in the Third World. Thus reinforced, the Soviet superpower can aspire to dominate the Arab world. This eventuality, which seems so unlikely today, nonetheless corresponds to deep-seated tendencies of the international system, to the decline of American imperialism, to a possible ascendency of the USSR and similar (internal) systems; in other words to the tendency towards centralisation of capital in the centres and the predominance of statist forms in the peripheries.

The inter-imperialist contradictions between Europe, Japan and the United States slip into the interstices of the gigantic struggle between the two superpowers. Europe can either play its own game, or can on the contrary reappear in the area only as a partner of the United States' new strategy. What will this choice depend on? Today, capitalist Europe has opted for the second of these choices, but if, thanks to the crisis, 'historical compromises' should bring a revisionist alliance to power in Southern Europe, the latter could intervene in the Arab world either in the wake of the USSR or even to further its own new imperialism.

In either case, there is little hope for Arab unity. For it is hardly likely that the Arab bourgeoisie will succeed in overcoming its internal contradictions, or that a section of this bourgeoisie will manage to impose itself as the leadership of the whole of the Arab world: the bourgeoisie is far too dependent on foreign alliances. As for the superpowers, they will obviously find it easier to dominate a dismembered Arab world.

THE CONDITIONS FOR SOCIALIST REVOLUTION IN THE ARAB WORLD

The third possibility is based on the perspective for socialism. It can be defined by its two essential characteristics: a break with the capitalist world system, and the establishing of popular power.

There can be no transition to socialism without a disengagement from the world capitalist system. All those who still uphold a linear vision of progress and consider that the development of the productive forces must necessarily precede the transformation of the relations of production must also accept the Trotskyist theses according to which socialism can only come from the developed capitalist world. The unequal development thesis is the exact opposite of this linear, mechanistic and economicist conception. It draws the conclusion from the facts of imperialism, namely that socialism begins on the periphery of the system, that the revolutions in the periphery cannot be treated as part of the ascendant cycle of rising capitalism, that they are not shameful bourgeois revolutions but stages in the socialist transformation of the world. Disengagement is thus not a matter of pure opportunism, far less an unfortunate necessity imposed by the belatedness of revolution in the West. It conditions the revolutionary breakthrough. In its renunciation of Western patterns of consumption and, to some extent, of Western technologies, it is a commitment to transcend them. This disengagement operates as a powerful force for liberation, allowing the people to understand in practical terms that neither these patterns of consumption nor these technologies are neutral. It makes it possible to affirm relations of production which, in their denial of these Western patterns, favour a development of the productive forces capable of overtaking that which capitalism has achieved. These socialist relations of production are the content of popular power. It is of course perfectly understandable that the revisionist thesis, which reduces social control of production to public ownership of the means of production, should also accept the linear evolutionist vision of a new class state.

The Arab communists have always insisted that socialism involved workers' control as well as public ownership, it is true. But they were not aware that workers' control is impossible without a thoroughgoing re-evaluation of the organisation of labour, of the distribution of tasks, of the separation of leadership or conceptual functions from the tasks of the rank and file. In other words they did not grasp that there can be no workers' control without challenging the dogma which argues that technologies are neutral reflections of the need to develop the productive forces; the truth, of course, is that these technologies only manifest this need on the basis of given relations of production. The erroneous formulations of revisionism are behind the failure of workers' self-management even in countries which have undergone socialist revolution, such as Yugoslavia. As long as it holds sway, the workers have little interest in management. All these fundamental issues are ignored by revisionist communism, including Arab communism.

Is the Arab world capable of launching itself on the road to socialism? There are considerable obstacles which militate against such a course. Firstly, there is its integration into the capitalist system, which is considerably more advanced than was the case in China, for example. The Arab world is already very urbanised; its petty bourgeoisie, a reactionary class integrated into the capitalist system, is very developed; its rural areas are dominated by kulaks who benefited from the bourgeois agrarian reforms; all this manifests itself in a profound de-culturalisation, a great moral and intellectual confusion, in other words, by all the signs of lumpen-Europeanisation. In this sense, oil — to the extent that it is the most powerful factor contributing to the Arab world's integration into the world capitalist system — has been a source of misfortunes, miseries and impotence for the Arab people.

At the level of the development of revolutionary consciousness, the radical critique of revisionism has hardly begun. Hope rests entirely on the fact that the several contradictions which dependent development has engendered can no longer be overcome.

Of course, if the Arab world manages to launch itself in this socialist direction, the stages and modalities of its transformation will reflect the specificities of the Arab context. Whilst the lessons of China are certainly universal in terms of the principles outlined above, this does not mean that there is a Chinese model which can be reproduced in the Arab world. Specific solutions will have to be found.

Let us look at the situation and perspectives in agriculture, for example. Major progress in agricultural productivity is inconceivable without heavy investment in irrigation and mechanisation. Furthermore the highly urbanised Arab world will have to develop relations between agriculture and industry different from those which characterise the Chinese strategy for transition. Within the capitalist perspective, there are two possible solutions to this problem. The first solution consists in neglecting agriculture and meeting the requirements for foodstuffs by exportation, of oil at first, then of manufactured products later. The second solution consists in financing the modernisation of an enclave agriculture from the same sources. Both these strategies tie the Arab world to the world system. It is clear that a solution to this problem envisaged from a socialist perspective would be based on strictly autocentric pan-Arab development. Industry, localised in the areas of lowest agricultural potential, would be used to develop agriculture in the areas with the highest potential, in the Sudan for example.

This kind of strategy leads to Arab unity. Not that this could be achieved immediately, of course. That would be neither necessary nor useful, in fact it would be dangerous. A long transition which respects regional particularities is a far better strategy. A collective mutual aid aimed at reinforcing the autonomy of the whole and the interdependence of its constituent states is the only road to popular and socialist Arab unity.

Breakaway strategies of this kind are practical possibilities in the Arab world. They would be greatly facilitated if the liberation of the Arab world was concomitant with the liberation of other areas of the Third World, notably Black Africa and the Indian sub-continent. In such a case, given the absence of any need to refer to the world system, original development projects for the building of socialism could turn the emancipation of peoples and the transcendence of capitalism from hopes into reality.

In all these perspectives, Egypt occupies a key position. Since the beginning of the 19th century, it has regained its status as the centre of the Arab world, the place where the fate of the area is decided. The Arab renaissance came from Egypt, as did all the great attempts at capitalist modernisation of the Arab world. The first of these goes back to Mohamed Ali, in the first half of the last century. It was broken by the European intervention. The second goes back to the khedives and the monarchy, who accepted imperialist domination and tried to develop the country within that context. This second attempt engendered the contradictions which led to Nasserism, itself a third attempt. Today, bogged down as it is in insoluble contradictions, Egypt stands in the way of a neo-imperialist solution and ruins the chances of the project which aims to find a new place for the Arab world in the capitalist international division of labour. Oil billions and the various neo-Nasserist confusions all come up against the insurmountable obstacle of the Egyptian people's silent but obstinate resistance.

Perhaps this sketch of a third possible outcome for the Arab world, based on its socialist transformation and unification, seems unrealistic, in view of the analysis which we have proposed as a means to understand what we do not hesitate to call the triple defeat of the Arab world's liberation movement. But it is not unrealistic. All the conditions are gathered for the appearance of an invincible revolutionary upsurge in the Arab world: a large concentrated and embattled proletariat, and vast impoverished peasant masses which are exploited and close to the proletariat. The bourgeoisie has gone bankrupt and the petty bourgeoisie which had led the movement till now has demonstrated its instability and its limits. But this same petty bourgeoisie, for all its pusillanimity when it led the movement as a class, has produced thousands of revolutionaries.

There are two pre-conditions if this potentiality is to become a reality. Firstly, a broad anti-imperialist front must be constituted. Secondly, the leadership of this front must be assumed by an ideologically and organisationally autonomous working class, in close alliance with the impoverished peasantry. Then the Arab working class, sole torch bearer of the Arab future, will be able to reach out to all the forces, both internal and external, which stand against imperialism; and it will be able to do so without losing its leadership of the movement. Then, and only then, a firmly grounded strategy will be able to employ flexible tactics, such as the Vietnamese have so clearly demonstrated.

REFERENCES AND NOTES

Foreword

1.   Samir Amin, *Unequal Development: An Essay on the Social Form-ations of Peripheral Capitalism*, (Monthly Review, 1976); *L'imperialisme et le developpement egal*, (Minuit, 1976); *Unequal Exchange and the Law of Value*, (Harvester, 1978); Samir Amin, Alexandre Faire, Mahmoud Hussein, Gustave Massiah, *La crise de l'imperialisme*, (Minuit, 1975).
2.   Hassan Riad, *L'Egypt nasserienne*, (Minuit, 1964); Mahmoud Hussein, *Class Conflict in Egypt: 1945-1970* (Monthly Review, 1974); Samir Amin, *Maghreb in the Modern World*, (Penguin).

Chapter 1

1.   Maxime Rodinson, *Muhammad* (Penguin, 1974).

Chapter 2

1.   See Moustapha Fahmy *La revolution de l'industrie en Egypte, et ses consequences sociales au XIXeme siecle (1800-1850)*, (Leiden: E.J. Brill, 1954); selected works of various authors' (including Jabarti) in *The Economic History of the Middle East 1800-1914*, ed. by C. Issawi, (University of Chicago Press, 1966).
2.   See Georges Antoios, *The Arab Awakening*, (in Arabic 1946).
3.   Ali Abdel Razek, *Islam and Sources of Power*, (in Arabic, Cairo, 1925).
4.   Works of Sayed Qotb; (in Arabic, Cairo, 1950).
5.   *Culture et developpement en Syrie et dans les pays arabes*, (Anthropos, 1969).

Chapter 4

1.   Fouad Raouf, 'Introduction a une etude de la revolution palestin-ienne'; *Travaux sur le capitalisme et l'economie politique, No. 9*, (Universite de Vincennes, Paris, 1973).
2.   See Mahmoud Hussein, *L'Egypte*, (Maspero, 1975).
3.   See Fred Halliday, *Arabia Without Sultans*, (Pelican, 1974).
4.   See Inga Brandell, *L'Algerie et les societes multinationales* (roneo) (Uppsala University, 1974); Jan Annerstedt and Rolf Gustavsson, *Towards a New International Economic Division of Labour*, (Rue Boghandel, 1975).
5.   See Mahammed Harbi, *Aux origines de F.L.N. — Le populisme revolutionnaire en Algerie*, (Paris, 1975); Kadar Ammoun, Christine Leucate, Jean-Jacques Moulin, *La vide algerienne*, (Maspero, 1974).

Chapter 5

1. See Karl Wittfogel, *Oriental Despotism*, (1964).

Chapter 6

1. See Samir Amin, *La crise de l'imperialisme, op. cit.*
2. See Michel Chatelus, *Strategie pour le Moyen-Orient*, (Canann-Levy, 1974).
3. Chatelus, *op. cit.*
4. For a critique of Rostow's thesis, see Samir Amin, *Unequal Development, op. cit;* For a new definition of the new international division of labour, see *La crise de l'imperialisme, op. cit.*

zed

ZED PRESS is a new socialist publisher of books on the Third World. Our first series are: Imperialism and Revolution, Women in the Third World, Africa, the Middle East and Asia.

Our books are both introductory texts and more advanced analyses of the complex forms of oppression which Third World revolutionary forces are struggling to overcome. Most of our authors use Marxism as their basis for coming to grips with political history, with the way the world is structured and with what the future holds. Our writers are people, many of whom are in active opposition to the forces of imperial oppression in its many local and international manifestations. We intend our authors to be equally from the Third World and from the West.

ZED PRESS is committed to taking radical literature out of the studies of the academics and into the hands of a much wider circle of intellectuals who feel the need to understand our contradiction and crisis-ridden world. We will encourage manuscripts which do this.

We aim to distribute ZED's books as widely as possible, especially in the Third World. We want to get our books directly to those involved in anti-imperialist struggles. We have a network of representatives, and are building up a direct mail order service to make our books accessible anywhere in the world. We are therefore willing to help other radical publishers in providing a more comprehensive distribution of their titles in the Third World, in addition to originating our own titles.

ZED PRESS is financially independent and not tied to any political faction. Our aim is to encourage broad debate in a Marxist and socialist framework, to promote radical knowledge and to build up a climate of opinion favourable to liberation everywhere.

Victor Kiernan

AMERICA: THE IMPERIAL RECORD
Two centuries of U.S. expansionism

This is the first book to discuss American imperialism from the
date of her political independence from Britain up to the present
time. Many books discuss particular phases, but none review the
entire record of US imperialism over two hundred years, and
there are none which set US expansion in the context of world
history.

THE AUTHOR is a mature and radical scholar who has been
studying imperialism for a number of years. He has taught in
India, and now is Professor of History at Edinburgh. Victor
Kiernan is well known for his book 'The Lords of Human Kind'.
His latest work succeeds in grasping the broad movements of
US history.

CONTENTS: The book is arranged in six parts: the early phase
of American history up to the Mexican War in 1846; the middle
decades of the 19th century; end of the 19th century to war
with Spain in 1898; the years before 1914; the interwar years;
and finally 1945 up to the present day.

Kiernan follows several themes: the settlers' military defeat of
the American Indians, and then the new American states' ongoing
relationship with these colonised peoples is compared with the
record of other imperialisms.

Each section of the book covers the major events of the period,
but Kiernan's work is not merely a narrative: he follows the
ideological developments through America's history. America's
outlook and policies have shifted in response to her internal
growth and external exigencies. Kiernan locates these ideological
shifts in literary and political writings of the time.

In an era when people in the Third World and the capitalist
countries are only too aware that America's influence today is
greater than any other powers has been before, Kiernan's book
is a timely exposition of the complex currents and deep historical
roots of US imperialism.

0 905762 18 5 Price: UK £6.95; Rest of world $12.95

Malcolm Caldwell

THE WEALTH OF SOME NATIONS
An Introduction to Political Economy

Caldwell's book introduces an exciting new perspective to the
study of political economy: the dependence of food production
on energy supplies on a world scale. He shows how food and
energy are fundamental to development and how, in the era of
food shortages in the Third World and energy crises in the West,
this basic equation underlying industrial society is at stake.

Caldwell's book penetrates the maze of material that has been
written on development, the Third World and ecological issues.
He reminds us that agriculture is the basis of all wealth and that
only the huge energy input needed to mechanise agriculture makes
industrialisation of an economy possible. Once this is understood
the inescapable importance of fossil fuels to Western economies
becomes clear. These fossil fuels are now being rapidly exhausted,
to the extent that the West's overdeveloped levels of consumption face inevitable reduction.

CONTENTS: Fossil Fuels and Entropy; Development and Underdevelopment in the Third World; Overdevelopment in the West;
Towards Homeostasis: Studies of the self-sufficient socialist
economies in Asia.

AUTHOR is a leading scholar in Asian studies. In this book he
uses his wide experience to evaluate possible alternative models
of development for the future, in particular those practised by
socialist China, North Korea and Indochina, which in his own
words: 'For the peoples of the Third World . . . hold out vistas
of far greater hopefulness than those to which we, in the rich
countries, so desperately cling as we grapple with the end of
imperialism.'

READERSHIP: it is highly suitable as an introductory text for
social scientists, politically concerned natural scientists and
environmentalists alike.

0 905762 01 0 Price: UK £5.00; Rest of World $10.00 (Hb)
0 905762 00 2 Price: UK £3.00; Rest of World $ 6.00 (Pb)

Imperialism Series

D. Wadada Nabudere

THE POLITICAL ECONOMY OF IMPERIALISM
Its theoretical and polemical treatment from mercantilist to multilateral Imperialism

This book is a major contribution to the body of political theory coming from Africa today. Using a rigorous application of Marxist-Leninist concepts, Nabudere gives a coherent analysis of the rise of early mercantilism, and shows how it inevitably developed through the different stages of the growth of capitalism to the present hegemony of finance capital. In the latter half of the book Nabudere calls to task the neo-Marxist theorists and reasserts the continuing validity of Lenin's great work on imperialism. This he achieves by relating the changes in imperialism which have taken place since World War II to Lenin's original theory.

HIS ARGUMENT: Nabudere's central tenet is that imperialism is the mechanism used by capital to overcome the tendency for the rate of profit to fall. Capital has to control the ratio of constant capital to variable capital and the prime means available has been to obtain cheap raw materials. This process sets up a crucial contradiction in the development of those economies in the Third World where the raw materials are produced: development of these economies is contrary to the interests of the already industrialised nations. This contradiction is today heightened by the repressive effects of finance capital. Throughout the author stresses that the changing forms of imperialism have been a necessary feature of Western capitalism's struggle to contain its own crisis.

Nabudere's analysis provides an excellent introduction to the process of world domination. Historically he covers the whole of the imperialist era, and reviews the theories of Luxemburg, Hilferding, Gundar Frank, and others. His elaborate survey of present day financial institutions, economic theories and power politics, in the era of U.S.A.'s multilateral strategy, transnational corporations and neo-colonialism, offers a firm basis for understanding international relations.

Published in association with Tanzania Publishing House for distribution in Africa.

0 905762 03 7 Price: £7.75; Rest of World $15.50

Belinda Probert

THE NORTHERN IRELAND CRISIS
A Study in Protestant Politics

Is the crisis in Northern Ireland simply a matter of a handful of gunmen terrorising the Northern Irish people, or is it much deeper, a consequence of the residue in Northern Ireland of Britain's longstanding imperial role? Probert's radical analysis of the political economy of Ireland goes to the very heart of the economy and politics of Irish society since the Act of Union in 1801. It can indeed claim to provide the reader with a coherent account of the basic forces out of which the present violence has grown.

THE ARGUMENT: Probert argues that the basis of the present struggle lies in the character of capital in Northern Ireland and present-day Eire. The principal contradiction underlying the struggle relates to the manner in which capital has changed. The result is the class nature of political organisation, despite its apparent religious nature, the peripheral character of Irish capitalism and the changing role of British imperialism.

Probert focuses primarily on the forces which led to the break-up of the old ruling families, the Unionist hegemony, who have ruled all Ireland up to Partition, and Northern Ireland till the mid 1960s. The book examines the changing nature of capital over the last 100 years, particularly the decline of local domestic capital and the rise of monopoly capital throughout the island. The author then examines the transformation of Anglo-Irish relations after World War II with the international decline of the British Empire. Finally, she deals in depth with the responses of the various sections of the Protestant community to the pressures for reform, which have followed in the wake of these structural changes in Ireland.

The joy of this book is how Probert's theoretical perspective allows her to make sense of the kaleidoscope of recent events with a clarity which is not lost in anecdote or unnecessary descriptive material. At the same time she succeeds in explaining the dilemmas and characteristics of the present situation, with sufficient detail to allow the reader to come to terms with the basis of the conflict.

0 905762 16 9 Price: UK £6.50; Rest of world $12. 50

Uri Davis

ISRAEL: UTOPIA INCORPORATED
A Study of Class, State and Corporate Kin Control

This counter-history of Zionism is an important political book.
It provides an integrated critique of the structure of Israeli society.
Written by an Israeli who was imprisoned as one of the first war
resisters, this book provides information on the internal mechanisms of the political and economic scene within Israel, which
few people outside are aware of.

This book asks: Who does Israel really belong to? Uri Davis's
answer is that Israeli state power has always been monopolised
by a ruling elite, relying on kinship as the principle of its recruitment and its self-perpetuation.

THE ARGUMENT: Davis shows how the reality of the early
struggle to establish a Jewish state in Israel has been concealed
by an ideology rooted in Jewish history. This ideology of Zionism
has been used to justify Israel's repressive policies towards the
indigenous inhabitants of the area. Davis argues that Zionism has
also perpetrated fictions, including the idea that the native Arab
population had voluntarily withdrawn from their villages after the
1948 war. He believes that the Zionist movement has misled
large sections of liberal and radical Western opinion, particularly
the United States, into supporting the Zionist effort as basically
an humanitarian and progressive endeavour. This has enabled
Israel to use war constantly to achieve its objectives, at the
expense of the working class and the Oriental Jews who have
been crippled through structural policies of economic exploitation and political subordination.

CONTENTS: The Moral Dilemma; The Origin of Zionism: anti-
Semitism, kibbutzim and moshavim; Oriental Jews: fear of
levantization, arrival of immigrants, cultural hostilities; Kinship
as History (with case studies); Israeli 'Socialism': South African
link, militarization of economy, who rules the Histadrut; Israel
and the U.S., The Future.

'Most original and most intriguing contribution to an understanding of Israeli society . . .' Events Magazine.

0 905762 12 6 Price: UK £5.00; Rest of World $10.00 (Hb)
0 905762 13 4 Price: UK £3.00; Rest of World $ 6.00 (Pb)

Claude Ake

REVOLUTIONARY PRESSURES IN AFRICA

This concise book is one of the most provocative to have come out of Africa in the 1970s.

THE CENTRAL ARGUMENT of Claude Ake's work is this: Revolutions against capitalism in Africa will constitute the new historic era that the continent is now entering. The author explains why this new era is upon us. The new black ruling classes have shown themselves incapable of leading the struggle against neo-colonial dependence effectively, or of correcting the distorted capitalist structures which imperialism has implanted. Out of this situation the material conditions and new class consciousness are growing that will make socialist revolution inevitable for Africa.

Claude Ake, who is a West African now teaching Social Science in Nigeria, presents a wide ranging and original analysis of modes of production in Africa, class structures, the ruling classes' reliance on Western theories of development, problems of surplus, state capitalism and their associated political and ideological forms. His clear handling of Marxist concepts to explain the African situation makes the book readily accessible to students and the general public alike.

We feel this book ought to take its place beside the works of other great African intellectuals such as Fanon, Cabral and Rodney.

CONTENTS. The Global Context: The struggle of 'proletarian' versus 'bourgeois' countries; consequences for Africa; growth of revolutionary political consciousness.

Neo-Colonial Dependence: The African bourgeoisie and neo-colonialism; case studies in economic indigenization in Nigeria, Kenya, Tanzania.

The Class Struggle: Africa's class structure; the African bourgeoisie as an obstacle to progress; the Western ideology of development; underdeveloped nature of capitalism in Africa; depoliticization as a bourgeois strategy; penetration of underdevelopment.

Ideological Containment: Colonial ideology, nationalist ideology, post-colonial ideology.

Dynamics of Social Forces: Conditions for transition to socialism; prospects for socialism in Africa; Africa's real choice.

0 905762 14 2 Price: UK £6.50; Rest of World $13.00

Baruch Hirson

SOWETO: THE ROOTS OF A REVOLUTION?

This is an analysis of the Soweto uprising by black South African students and workers in 1976/77. The author is a South African revolutionary and social scientist who has been gaoled during the liberation struggle. He outlines the economic roots and analyses the key events of the uprising. He also provides a clear and constructively critical view of the student's Black Consciousness ideology.

CONTENTS: This book's historical account goes right up to the regime's draconian, but desperate, attempts at repression in October 1977. The author shows Soweto as the latest manifestation of black South Africans' long struggle to reject white racism. Because Black Consciousness ideology is the creation of a subjected intelligentsia and operates primarily at the psychological level, however, it has not analysed the nature of capitalism sufficiently to respond to the pressing economic demands of the black working class and rural proletariat.

The book provides important insights for those who support the South African revolution.

(In preparation)

Ann and Neva Seidman

US MULTINATIONALS IN SOUTHERN AFRICA

This book is on the roles which US multinational companies and banks play in fortifying racist exploitation and oppression in Southern Africa. The roles of companies based in Western Europe are also analysed, as are those of the US Government and American labour unions.

The Seidmans chart the growth of South African industry, explain the advent of state capitalism and show how manufacturing has overtaken mining as the leading economic sector.

South Africa's penetration into, and domination over, the economies of other African countries in the region is also exposed.

Price: UK £4.95 (Not available in Africa and North America)

Asia Series

David L. Elliott

THAILAND: ORIGINS OF MILITARY RULE

Vietnam, Cambodia, Laos — all these South-east Asian countries have since 1965 experienced internal revolutions which have launched them on paths away from capitalism. Thailand, the largest country in the South-east Asian mainland and lying at its very hub, now also faces the 'spectre of communism', to use Marx's celebrated phrase. David Elliott's book is the first major Marxist analysis to explain why Thailand has so persistently been ruled by the military, and why its military regime is now more gravely threatened than ever before by the revolutionary forces in the jungles of the North-east and South.

HIS ARGUMENT: Elliott's central thrust is to explain how Thailand's political economy has changed under the impact of European imperialism from the Asiatic mode of production based on rice cultivation, which existed prior to the early 19th century, to its present state of underdeveloped capitalism. Changes in the economic base, in the class structure and in the nature and role of the state over the past 150 years are analysed with empirical care.

CONTENTS: The author examines the evolution of Thailand's political economy to show the roots of military rule within the society. Introduction by Malcolm Caldwell (South-east Asian specialist at the London School of Oriental and African Studies) The Thai Rice Economy: An Asiatic mode of production; Early Underdevelopment: Prelude to Military Rule — foundation of the state, class formation, new economic structures and dependence patterns. Monarchism to Militarism: Seizure of the Rice Economy — 1932 coup and the military regime up to 1960s, economic changes and class formation in these periods; Class Struggles and U.S. Imperialism to 1976 — contradictions of underdeveloped capitalism, foreign investment and U.S. military imperialism, growth of a working class.

This book will be invaluable reading for all those interested in Asia, Imperialism and Underdevelopment, and in the Marxist theory of transition from one mode of production to another.

0 905762 10 X Price: UK £5.95; Rest of World $12.95

OTHER BOOKS AVAILABLE THROUGH ZED PRESS

Jan Annerstedt and Rolf Gustavsson

TOWARDS A NEW INTERNATIONAL ECONOMIC DIVISION OF LABOUR

A useful contribution to the theory of imperialism. Already translated into Swedish and Italian. It argues that Western multi-national corporations' monopoly over technology is now the central mechanism perpetuating dependence and imperialist relationships. Fully documented with much empirical material.

87 87474 19 8 Price: UK £1.95; Rest of World $3.75 (Available only outside Scandinavia)

Arlene Eisen Bergman

WOMEN IN VIETNAM

Uplifting account of Vietnamese women's oppression and struggle for liberation, from earliest times, through French colonial exploitation and US military aggression to present-day socialist reconstruction. Vietnamese personal accounts, poems and photos combine with the analytic history. Important inspiration to women's movements in the Third World.

0 914750 02 X Price: US £2.70; Rest of World $5.40 (Available only outside North America)

Ernest Mandel

FROM CLASS SOCIETY TO COMMUNISM
An Introduction to Marxism

An introduction to the basic arguments and concepts of Marxist theory. Specially written for people who want to understand capitalism and imperialism today, and how to change them. The author, Ernest Mandel, is both a major Marxist theoretician and a committed political activist.

Price: $10.50 (Hb); $3.95 (Pb)
(Available only in Africa, Asia and the Middle East)

Peoples Press Angola Book Project

WITH FREEDOM IN THEIR EYES

A short photo-plus-text history of Angola compiled after MPLA's victory in the Civil War. The simple text, drawings and photographic composition make this an ideal introduction for all who want to learn about the Angolan people's struggle for liberation.

0 914750 08 9 Price: UK £2.50; Rest of World $5.00 (Available only outside North America)

Peoples Press

OUR ROOTS ARE STILL ALIVE:
The Story of the Palestinian People

A superb introduction to the Palestinian struggle from the initial Zionist penetration up to and including the Lebanese Civil War. Immensely readable and with many illustrations and photos. Ideal for the general reader.

Price: UK £2.95; Rest of World $5.95 (Available only outside North America)

Bonnie Mass

POPULATION TARGET
The Political Economy of Population Control in Latin America

Contraceptive devices are *the* revolutionary change to have affected women's lives in the last 25 years. A progressive measure in the West in that women can now control their own reproduction, in Third World countries Birth Control techniques have been used by the most reactionary forces of imperialism to prevent the multiplication of the peoples of the Third World. POPULATION TARGET is the key work which explores this new dimension of imperialist aggression.

Price: UK £2.95 (Not available in North America)